RENAISSANCE

Medal showing Bramante's design for the new St. Peter's

Fragment of a world map of 1537

Model of Leonardo's flying machine

The Wilton Diptych, c.1395

Fra Angelico, *The Deposition*, c.1440–45

Laocoön, 2nd–1st century B.C.

Leonardo da Vinci's drawing of *Vitruvian Man*, c.1487

Ghiberti's self-portrait, from the Baptistery doors, 1425–52

DK EYEWITNESS BOOKS

RENAISSANCE

ALISON COLE

Joachim Patenier,
*St. Jerome in
a Rocky
Landscape,*
1515

Titian, *The Assumption
and Coronation of
the Virgin,*
1516–18

Ghiberti, *Joseph in
Egypt,* from the
Baptistery doors,
1425–52

Masaccio, *The Expulsion,* c.1427

Dorling Kindersley

Michelangelo,
Moses, c.1515

Raphael, *Portrait of Baldassare Castiglione*, c.1514–15

Andrea del Castagno,
The Youthful David, c.1450

Dorling Kindersley

LONDON, NEW YORK, AUCKLAND, DELHI,
JOHANNESBURG, MUNICH, PARIS and SYDNEY

For a full catalog, visit

 www.dk.com

Editor Luisa Caruso
Art editor Tracy Hambleton-Miles
Assistant editor Peter Jones
Assistant designer Simon Murrell
Senior editor Gwen Edmonds
Managing editor Sean Moore
Managing art editor Toni Kay
US editor Laaren Brown
Picture researchers Julia Harris-Voss,
Jo Evans
DTP designer Zirrinia Austin
Production controller Meryl Silbert

This Eyewitness ® Book has been conceived by
Dorling Kindersley Limited and Editions Gallimard

Published in the United States by
DK Publishing, Inc.
375 Hudson Street
New York, New York 10014
4 6 8 10 9 7 5

Library of Congress Cataloging-in-Publication Data
Cole, Alison.
Renaissance / written by Alison Cole.
p. cm. — (Eyewitness Books)
Includes index.
1. Art, Renaissance. I. Title. II. Series.
N6370.C55 2000   93-21264
709′.02′4—dc20   CIP
ISBN 0-7894-6175-7 (pb)   ISBN 0-7894-5582-X (hc)

Color reproduction by Colourscan, Singapore
Printed in China by Toppan Printing Co. (Shenzhen) Ltd.

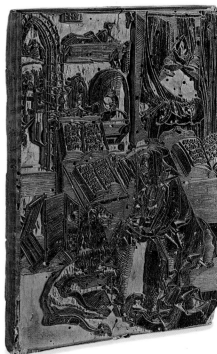

Woodblock of Albrecht Dürer's
St. Jerome in His Study, 1492

Reliquary containing
St. Dominic's skull

Hugo van der Goes, *Portinari Altarpiece*, c.1476–78

Contents

Albrecht Dürer,
St. Anthony in Front of the City, 1519

What is the Renaissance?

THE LABEL "RENAISSANCE" (French: "rebirth") is usually applied to a period in the history of Western Europe stretching from the early 14th century to the mid to late 16th century. In writings of the time, however, the term was used more specifically to describe a movement – the new spirit of rebirth in art and literature. It first applied to the revived study of classical learning, popularized by the Italian poet and Latin scholar Petrarch (1304–74), who rejected the Middle Ages as a period of "darkness"; later Erasmus of Rotterdam (c.1469–1536) welcomed new translations of ancient texts and a "purer literature." The idea of rebirth in art was developed by the Florentine art historian Giorgio Vasari (1511–74). He claimed, in his *Lives of the Most Excellent Painters, Sculptors, and Architects* (1550), that art had been reborn in Italy in about 1250 and had progressed through "childhood" and "youth" to its 16th-century maturity. It is this self-conscious awareness of being part of something new and superior that gives a confident and cohesive character to the Renaissance period. Now, with the advantage of historical perspective, the Renaissance is seen as building on, rather than breaking with, its medieval heritage, and northern Europe is considered as important as Italy in the development of new ideals and techniques. North and south of the Alps, there was a new interest in naturalism: to the Italians, their ancient Roman past held the key to truth and nature in art; the Flemish found truth in the observation of nature. The interchange between these two approaches is one of the determining factors of Renaissance style.

THE TAZZA FARNESE
The Renaissance Italians idealized the classical past, seeing their own period as a second Golden Age. Antique works, like this Alexandrian agate bowl (2nd–1st century B.C.), were prized for their techniques (once lost) and were often copied. Botticelli adapted the mythological figures of the Etesian winds, who ensured the Nile's fertility, for his *Birth of Venus* (below).

THE BIRTH OF VENUS
Sandro Botticelli; c.1486; 70 x 180¼ in (175 x 275 cm); tempera on canvas
This famous mythological picture by Sandro Botticelli (pp. 32–33) illustrates the birth of Venus, goddess of love – and the rebirth of the ancient ideal of beauty in the Early Renaissance. Botticelli, like earlier artists, has borrowed the pose of a Roman antique statue, the *Medici Venus* (p. 19), for his Venus and altered it to contemporary Florentine tastes. He has refined and simplified all the figures, enhancing these effects by depicting long, flowing hair and fluttering draperies. The rhythmic forms of Gothic art – the style of medieval northern Europe (p. 63) – are fused with the styling of ancient Roman reliefs. A similar mingling of medieval and ancient influences appears in much of Early Renaissance art.

ENGLAND

London •

Paris

NAVARRE

ARAGON

CASTILE

Boundary of the Holy Roman Empire

Amsterdam

twerp

ssels

NDERS

Cologne

SAXONY

HOLY ROMAN EMPIRE

BURGUNDY

Nuremberg

Augsburg

Basel

DUCHY OF
MILAN

MANTUA

REPUBLIC OF
VENICE

Milan

Verona

Venice

Padua

SAVOY

Genoa

Ferrara

Bologna

DUCHY OF
FERRARA

DUCHY OF
MODENA

gnon

Pisa

Florence

Urbino
Arezzo

REPUBLIC
OF GENOA

Siena

Perugia

REPUBLIC OF
FLORENCE

PAPAL
STATES

DUCHY OF
PIOMBINO

REPUBLIC
OF SIENA

Rome

Naples

KINGDOM OF
NAPLES

SARDINIA

SICILY

A political map
of c.1450 showing
the main artistic
centers in Italy and
northern Europe

SELF-PORTRAIT
*Albrecht Dürer; 1500; 67 x 49 in
(170 x 124.5 cm); oil on canvas*

One of the driving forces for
change in the Renaissance was the
growing professionalization of the
artist. Artists won recognition as
creative innovators rather than
skilled craftsmen like carpenters
or tailors. They consolidated their
new social and economic status by
developing greater skills, such as
the mathematical techniques of
perspective (p. 28) and proportion
(p. 30), and composing theoretical
treatises. Painting, sculpture, and
architecture were gradually seen
as part of the liberal arts, and the
idea of the accomplished "universal
man" developed. The greatest
figure of the Northern Renaissance,
the German artist Albrecht Dürer
(pp. 40–41), was very conscious of
his own artistic status. He painted
this solemn self-portrait "in the
manner of Christ" to acknowledge
his "God-given" creative powers.
However, the transformation of
the artist's status occurred earlier
in Italy than in northern Europe.
When Dürer visited Italy in 1505–6,
he wrote back to his Nuremberg
correspondent : "here I am a gentleman, at home I am a parasite."

CHRIST AS RULER OF THE UNIVERSE
Dürer's *Self-portrait* has the majesty
of this Byzantine mosaic of Christ
(c.1190) in Monreale Cathedral,
Sicily. In the Middle Ages,
Italy was dominated by
the art of the Greek
Byzantine Empire, but
Renaissance Italians
thought it "crude" in
contrast to naturalistic
ancient Roman art.

*The Virgin's
idealized beauty
suggests her
spiritual purity*

PIETA
*Michelangelo; c.1498–1500;
height: 5 ft 9 in (1.74 m); marble*

This monumental sculpture was
made by the High Renaissance
master Michelangelo (pp. 54–55)
for a French cardinal, who specified
that it should be "the most beautiful
work in marble that exists today in
Rome." A *pietà* (Italian: "pity") is a
Northern medieval subject in
which the Virgin mourns her
dead Son. Michelangelo's
sculpture is the first Italian
version of the theme. It
shows the dead Christ
lying across the Virgin's
lap, and reflects a
Renaissance tendency,
inspired by the work of
the Greek philosopher
Plato, to idealize the
human form.

Renaissance centers

The Renaissance covers such a vast
sweep of time, and embraces so broad a
geographical area, that it is now divided
into manageable periods. The "Early
Renaissance" usually refers to Italian
art in Tuscany in about 1400 to 1500,
centering on the city-state of Florence
and the work of artists like Giotto,
Masaccio, Donatello, and Botticelli.
The "High Renaissance" relates
to art in Papal Rome, Florence,
and Venice, from about 1500
to 1540/80, focusing on
Michelangelo, Raphael,
Leonardo (who bridges the
Early and High Renaissance),
and Titian. The "Northern
Renaissance" encompasses
the art of the countries
in northern Europe (the
"North"), about 1400 to
1550, including artists as
diverse as Dürer from
Nuremberg and van
Eyck from Bruges.

The impact of Giotto

THE FLORENTINE GIOTTO DI BONDONE (c.1267–1337) was celebrated in his lifetime for the revolutionary naturalism of his new style. What so impressed Giotto's contemporaries was the emotional intensity and dramatic realism of his art. The famous poet Dante (p. 12) heralded him as foremost among painters, while the writer Boccaccio praised him for bringing the art of painting "back to light" after centuries of darkness. Giotto was credited with translating what was held to be the "rude manner" of the Byzantine era (p. 7) into the natural style that was then associated with ancient Roman art. This is clearly displayed in the best-preserved of his works, the great cycle of wall paintings in the Arena Chapel, Padua, which was executed in the popular medium of fresco (p. 63). Giotto's use of monumental human forms to tell stories simply and dramatically set an example for artists from Masaccio (pp. 18–19) to Michelangelo (pp. 54–55).

MEDIEVAL CONVENTIONS
This stained-glass window from Cologne Cathedral (1280) is an example of early storytelling in art. It shows the Annunciation, when the Angel Gabriel tells the Virgin that she will "conceive and bear a Son." The Annunciation was first portrayed in Gothic church art, using easily recognizable gestures, symbols – such as the dove of the Holy Spirit – and inscriptions.

THE GOLDEN LEGEND
Many images from the lives of the Virgin and saints were based on stories from *The Golden Legend* (left), written by Jacobus da Voragine in the 13th century.

THE ARENA CHAPEL
The Arena Chapel was built for the wealthy Italian merchant Enrico Scrovegni in his home city of Padua. It was dedicated to the Annunciation, and soon after its completion, the young Giotto was commissioned to decorate it (c.1305) with scenes from the lives of the Virgin and Christ. The vividly colored stories, surrounded by painted frames, are arranged in three tiers above pairs of virtues and vices, which are painted to look like statues (far right).

The Meeting at the Golden Gate

GIOTTO DI BONDONE *c.1306; 78¾ x 72¾ in (200 x 185 cm); fresco*
In this moving scene from the Arena Chapel, Giotto shows the meeting of Joachim and Anna (the future parents of the Virgin) before the Golden Gate of Jerusalem – a story related in *The Golden Legend*. Joachim has had a revelation while in the wilderness; his wife, Anna, has also been visited by an angel and told that she will bear a child. Returning to tell Anna, Joachim is met by his wife, and their kiss – set dramatically in the front plane of the picture – symbolizes the moment of the Virgin's Immaculate Conception.

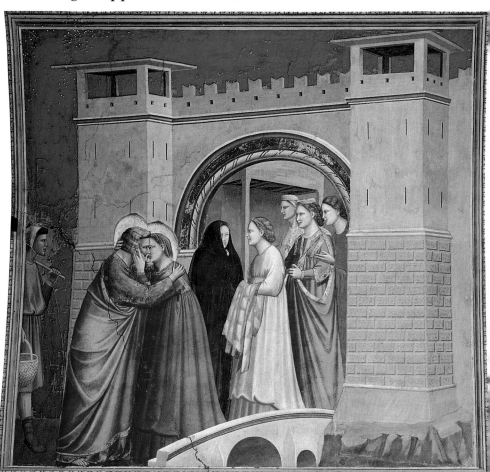

Detail of Joachim and Anna, from *The Meeting at the Golden Gate* (below left)

Detail of Christ and Judas, from *The Betrayal of Christ* (below)

MOTIONS OF THE MIND
Giotto's use of facial expression and gesture gives his figures immense psychological power. The tenderness of Joachim and Anna's embrace (far left) is expressed by their overlapping forms and gently encircling hands. Both lean forward and their eyes meet in an intense gaze of shared joy and suffering. In the *Betrayal* (left; below), Judas's taut arm is disguised by drapery. His lips are pursed, his eyes shrouded by his forehead – the antithesis of Christ, who meets his treachery with a calm, steady gaze. The soldiers, pressed between their profiles, add to the dramatic tension.

CHRISTIAN MORALITY
This toppling figure symbolizes the vice of Inconstancy and is one of the series of virtues and vices along the lower wall. Such figures were popular in medieval painting and sculpture, and were used by the church to give shape to abstract moral ideas. The scene of the Last Judgment often accompanies them as a moral warning (Giotto painted one on the entrance wall).

GIOTTO'S NARRATIVE MASTERPIECE
Giotto's mosaic of the *Navicella* (Italian: "little ship"), which decorated the old St. Peter's Basilica in Rome (p. 51), was praised for the diversity of its poses: each expresses "a disturbed mind." It was later damaged and is now best shown in engravings (left).

The Betrayal of Christ
GIOTTO DI BONDONE *c.1306;*
78¾ x 72¾ in (200 x 185 cm); fresco
This scene from the life of Christ in the Arena Chapel illustrates the moment when Christ is betrayed to his enemies by his disciple Judas. As Christ stands among soldiers, Judas encircles him with his cloak and identifies him with a kiss of greeting. As was customary, Giotto has included another episode within the scene – that of St. Peter cutting off the ear of the High Priest's servant. The High Priest is shown directing the gaze of the viewer with his pointing finger.

Painting in Siena

THE ART OF THE ITALIAN CITY-STATE of Siena developed its own particular style in the 14th century. It was dominated by Duccio di Buoninsegna (active 1278–1319), who had as great an impact on Sienese and French painting as his contemporary Giotto had on Florentine art. Duccio looked to Italy's Byzantine tradition (p. 7), combining its bold linear style, splendid coloring, and surface patterns with a new human intimacy. His followers and pupils, among them Ambrogio Lorenzetti (active 1319–48) and Simone Martini (active 1315–44), built on his stylish innovations. Lorenzetti created naturalistic images filled with anecdotal detail, while Martini, serving at the papal court in Avignon, produced works of great ornament and opulence. Later, such minute observation and decorative elegance gave rise to an alternative Renaissance style known as "International Gothic" (pp. 16–17).

SIENA'S CATHEDRAL
Between 1250 and 1350, Siena Cathedral was radically enlarged: the improvements included a new dome, a splendid new facade by Giovanni Pisano (p. 19), the bell tower, and a refurbished interior. After Siena's unexpected victory in battle over Florence in 1260, the Cathedral became the focus of ritual celebration and thanksgiving.

A reconstruction of Duccio's *Maestà*

The Annunciation (right)

THE ANNUNCIATION
Duccio di Buoninsegna; 1308–11;
17 x 17¼ in (43.2 x 43.8 cm); tempera on panel
This small panel is part of a vast double-sided altarpiece, made by Duccio and his workshop for Siena Cathedral, known as the *Maestà* (an image of the Virgin "in majesty"). In June 1311, the altarpiece was carried in joyful procession from Duccio's workshop to the Cathedral, astounding the crowds with its size and splendor. In 1771, the altarpiece was dismantled and several of its panels were sold abroad. The reconstruction (left) shows its front. The Virgin and Child are enthroned in majesty in the center, and scenes from the life of the Virgin (including episodes from Christ's childhood) appear above and below: *The Annunciation* begins the narrative cycle on the *predella* (Italian: "plinth"; p. 63). The back was painted in similar fashion, with more than 30 scenes from the life of Christ.

ALLEGORY OF GOOD GOVERNMENT
Ambrogio Lorenzetti; 1338;
7 ft 10 in x 46 ft (2.40 x 14 m); fresco
Siena's great town hall – the Palazzo Pubblico – shared center stage with the Cathedral. Its rooms were decorated with images ranging from successful military campaigns and disgraced rebels to *maestàs*. For the Peace Room, Lorenzetti painted his famous *Allegory of Good and Bad Government. The Effect of Good Government in the City and Its Countryside* (right) faithfully illustrates city statutes (for example, no coats of arms were to decorate the outsides of buildings), while the figure of Security, holding a criminal on the gallows, floats in the sky. Lorenzetti presents a vision of a well-governed city and countryside, where the nobility, merchants, and laborers go about their tasks. It is also an astonishingly naturalistic picture of Siena, the Arbia Valley, and the main road to Rome.

THE ANNUNCIATION

Simone Martini and Lippo Memmi; 1333; 104¼ x 120 in (265 x 305 cm); tempera on panel

In 1333, Simone Martini painted his own altarpiece for Siena Cathedral, assisted by his brother-in-law, Lippo Memmi. It depicts the Annunciation: this was the first time that the subject had been chosen to be the main image of an altarpiece. The Angel Gabriel's words to the Virgin, "Hail thou that art full of grace, the Lord is with thee" – which represent the moment of Christ's Incarnation – are embossed in Latin on the gold background. Martini and Memmi have created a pious image of sophisticated grace, using the opulence of the materials as an expression of spiritual splendor. As the Virgin shies away from the divine messenger, the naturalism of the scene is also clear.

PATTERNED MOTIFS
Martini was the first to use elaborate motif punches, rather than ring punches (below right), to decorate gold. As this detail shows, the haloes are inscribed with compasses or dividers and the gold is stamped with motifs. These patterns would shimmer in candlelight, giving a supernatural aura to the image.

The checks on the Angel's cloak emphasize its natural movement

The vase holds white lilies – a symbol of the Virgin's purity

The simulated marble floor enhances the rich effect

MAKING PUNCHED DECORATION
After the painting surface has been gilded (beaten gold leaf is laid over bole, a reddish brown clay, and polished with a burnisher), punched designs are made by holding the punch upright on the burnished gold leaf, then tapping sharply but softly with a hammer (left). The punch should produce an indent in the gold and its underlying preparatory surface, without breaking the film of thin gold leaf.

PUNCHING TOOLS
The Sienese developed the taste for punched gold ornament in panel painting, and exported tools to Florence. While modern punching tools (left) are made of cast metal, all but the simplest early Italian punches seem to have been cut by hand, so that each was unique.

Renaissance Florence

THE WEALTHY CITY REPUBLIC of Florence nurtured some of the most spectacular accomplishments of the Renaissance. Despite the loss of half its population in the plagues of 1340 and 1348, and the turbulence of warfare, popular uprisings, and political conspiracies, 15th-century Florence prospered. Governed as an independent commune by rich merchant families and guilds (trade associations; p. 63), the city was renowned for its tradition of liberty, its financial and political astuteness, and its superior craft skills. Under the patronage of the famous Medici family (1434–94), the easy exchange of ideas between politicians, artists, and scholars continued, and Florence entered a period of unrivaled cultural vitality. Pride in its achievements manifested itself in an ambitious building program, which aimed to make the city a model of beauty, order, and harmony.

VIEW OF FLORENCE
By the 15th century, Florence had absorbed the territory of many of its hostile neighbors, becoming the largest city in Europe. Surrounded by beautiful Tuscan countryside and protected by fortified walls, it nevertheless led a precarious existence. This map shows how the city is divided by the River Arno and is dominated by the dome of the Cathedral, which was to become a symbol of Florence's civic fortitude.

A marble bust of Brunelleschi, acclaimed as the "most famous Florentine architect"

PHILIPPI BRVNELLESCHI
FLORENTINI ARCHITECTI
CELEBERRIM EFFIGIES
OB·AN·SAL·M·CCCCXLIIII

BUST OF BRUNELLESCHI
Filippo Brunelleschi (1377–1446) first trained as a goldsmith, like his Florentine contemporaries Donatello and Ghiberti (pp. 14–15). He turned to sculpture but, after losing a competition for the new Florence Baptistery doors (p. 14) to Ghiberti, devoted himself to architecture. The huge dome of Florence Cathedral is his towering achievement.

THE CATHEDRAL DOME
Brunelleschi (right) designed a dome (1420–36) to crown the 14th-century cathedral of Santa Maria del Fiore: it had remained incomplete, with a huge octagonal opening that posed enormous construction problems. Although Brunelleschi went to Rome with the sculptor Donatello (p. 14) to study classical buildings, the dome is largely Gothic in character, built around a self-supporting masonry of eight main ribs.

The lantern admits light into the interior; it was completed after Brunelleschi's death by Michelozzo

Ribs are visible on the exterior

ENGINEERING INNOVATION
Brunelleschi invented a hoisting machine with pulleys (above): the masons no longer had to carry materials to the dome's staggering heights. Citizens were forbidden to hitch a ride on this unique machine.

The complexity of the 14th-century Cathedral contrasts with the simple, harmonious structure of the dome

CHURCH OF SANTO SPIRITO, RIGHT AISLE
In 1436, Brunelleschi designed the Church of Santo Spirito, which movingly expresses the ideals of the Early Renaissance. Here, the lofty Corinthian columns and niches faithfully copy antique examples. These Roman elements are combined in simple new geometric relationships, based on human proportions (pp. 30–31), to give a sense of order, space, and serenity.

THE TORNABUONI CHAPEL
The prosperity and prestige of Florence's ruling families lay at the heart of the city's artistic activities. This chapel, in the great Dominican Church of Santa Maria Novella, was owned by the Tornabuoni family, who were linked to the illustrious Medici family through marriage. Giovanni Tornabuoni, the head of the Medici bank and treasurer to Pope Sixtus IV, chose the popular painter Domenico Ghirlandaio (1449–94) to decorate his chapel with scenes from the lives of the Virgin and St. John the Baptist.

A Latin inscription adorns the classical temple

The Angel Appearing to Zacharias (detail)
DOMENICO GHIRLANDAIO
1485–90; fresco
Ghirlandaio's frescoes in Santa Maria Novella give a vivid insight into the political life of Florence in the late 15th century. This detail shows how a religious event has been transformed into a hymn to Florence's prosperity. Here, members of the Tornabuoni family are portrayed as "witnesses"; portraits of the leading scholars of the Tornabuoni/Medici circle appear elsewhere. The temple behind bears the inscription (detail, above left) of the fresco cycle's completion: "In the year 1490, when the most glorious city, renowned for its wealth, victories, arts, and architecture, enjoyed salubrity and peace."

SYMBOLS OF THE COMMUNE
The medieval Palazzo Vecchio, which was the seat of the Republican government, is adorned with the coats of arms of the commune (above), city wards, and public offices.

The famous symbol of the Florentine lily (center) was adopted in the latter part of the 13th century.

This 16th-century plaster bust of Machiavelli is by an unknown Florentine master

DANTE STANDING BEFORE FLORENCE
Domenico di Michelino; 1465; fresco
Florence's proud literary tradition dates from the time of the poet Dante (1265–1321), the narrative writer Boccaccio (1313–75), and the scholar and poet Petrarch (p. 6). This painting of Dante with his famous poem, *The Divine Comedy*, was placed in Florence Cathedral after the town of Ravenna had refused to return the poet's precious remains.

THE POLITICIAN MACHIAVELLI
The political writer Niccolò Machiavelli (1469–1527) witnessed the fall of the Florentine Republic in 1512. He had been an active member of the Republican regime, and spent his enforced retirement analyzing the egotistical ways of humanity and the ruthless realities of political power. Machiavelli also insisted on the preeminence of Florence by championing Florentine Italian as the language of the whole of Italy. These ideas were eloquently expressed in his writings, the most famous being *The Prince*.

Early Renaissance sculpture

IN FLORENTINE SCULPTURE of the early 15th century, the rapid pace of innovation was dictated by an atmosphere of open competition and rivalry. The independent associations of masters that represented the trades and professions – the guilds – vied with one another in their decoration of civic buildings. The sculptors based their style – especially in the field of relief, when the sculpture projected from a background – on Greco-Roman sculpture, the most visible evidence of their ancient heritage. The North, however, led the way toward a more majestic figure style, infusing sculpted forms with lively realism. The Florentine sculptor Lorenzo Ghiberti (1378–1455) even claimed that his style was derived from the work of a goldsmith in Cologne.

THE MOSES FOUNTAIN
Claus Sluter; 1395–1406; height:
6 ft (1.83 m); wood with polychrome
This huge work by the Burgundian sculptor Claus Sluter (d.1405/6) was once part of a cloister. The massive individualized figures of prophets reveal a realism new to Northern art

Ghiberti's Baptistery doors

Ghiberti spent most of his career working on two pairs of doors for Florence's Baptistery, a church opposite the Cathedral. He had just completed the North doors (1401–25), drawing on his expertise as a goldsmith to master bronze techniques, when the Guild of Cloth Importers commissioned a second set (1425–52). Now Ghiberti stunned his contemporaries with his new compositional and perspective skills (pp. 28–29).

THE GATES OF PARADISE
Ghiberti's East doors (these are replicas – the originals have been removed to a museum) were so admired by later sculptors that Michelangelo called them the "Gates of Paradise." There were originally meant to be 28 panels illustrating Old Testament episodes, but Ghiberti reduced these to ten by skillfully incorporating several events into each scene.

FRAMED PORTRAIT
This wry self-portrait of Ghiberti looms out of one of the small roundels in the frame of the door.

JOSEPH IN EGYPT
This panel of *Joseph in Egypt*, from Ghiberti's doors, illustrates his striking use of three or more planes of perspective in one scene. The graceful figures mostly inhabit the front plane; some move through the immense architecture in the middle plane; and the background dissolves into a convincing spatial vista (in the manner of Donatello's relief, below right).

THE SCULPTOR'S ART
This detail forms the right-hand portion of a relief by the Florentine sculptor Nanno di Banco (c.1374–1421). It shows a stonemason carefully measuring proportions and a sculptor chiseling a figure, with his mallet ready on one side. The relief is at the base of a niche dedicated to the Stonemason's Guild on the Florentine guild church of Or San Michele. Each of the guilds – from the Linen Drapers to the Armorers – was given its own niche, which it had to fill with a statue. Due to the threat of invasion, the guilds were pressured to fulfill this obligation quickly: the sculptures were completed within 20 years and display the skills of the foremost sculptors of the day

St. George

DONATELLO 1415–17;
height: 6 ft 10 in (2.09 m); marble

Donatello (c.1386–1466) established his reputation as the greatest sculptor in Italy with this statue of *St. George*, made for a niche on Or San Michele. St. George was the patron saint of the Guild of Armorers and Swordmakers, in whose niche he stood. The figure is infused with a dramatic inner life (notice the furrowed brow and sensitive features) and a dynamic alertness: each muscle is taut, the shield rests momentarily on its point, and the hands have the tension of readiness in repose.

The armor is carefully described

The corroded metal of the sword's socket is just visible

MISSING WEAPON
The clenched left hand still holds a socket, which is stained with corroded metal (detail, above). This shows that the saint was originally equipped with a metal sword (fashioned by the swordmakers, Donatello's patrons). Pointing out at the viewer, into the street, it would have enhanced the statue's realistic impact.

Drill holes at the back of the head indicate that St. George once had a helmet

This panel is shown in detail below

CANTORIA
Luca della Robbia; 1431–38; 10 ft 9 in x 18 ft 4 in (3.28 x 5.60 m); marble
This beautiful marble *Cantoria* (Italian: "singing gallery"), by Luca della Robbia (1400–82), was one of the most popular works of the Early Renaissance. It was originally positioned above the door of the North Sacristy in Florence Cathedral, overlooking the high altar. Children and infants, who sing and play music, are presented in a paneled frieze. They illustrate verses from Psalm 150, in which God is praised "with the sound of the trumpet ... with stringed instruments and organs."

DETAIL OF CANTORIA
Although Luca della Robbia's relief panels are based on Roman examples, they have a natural charm and vivacity that reflect Florentine tastes of the time. Della Robbia has created an ideal of grace through the flowing lines of the draperies and the smooth polish of the sculpted forms. His *Cantoria* faced another by Donatello, in which the figures seem almost violent by comparison.

ST. GEORGE AND THE DRAGON
Donatello's most revolutionary innovation lies in the marble relief beneath the statue of *St. George*. In conventional relief sculpture, rounded figures were raised from a level back panel (far left). Donatello, however, has flattened his forms and made the background dissolve into space, light, and air.

SCULPTING TOOLS
The carving tools of the sculptor have changed little over the centuries. Chisels were struck with a mallet: the pointed chisel chipped off large pieces of stone, shaping the figure, and the flat chisel was used on the surface.

15

The courtly style

At the end of the 14th century, Gothic art north and south of the Alps acquired an international flavor as communications between European courts improved. A new style, which is known as International Gothic, flourished all over Western Europe in the period between 1380 and 1430, spreading from center to center as trade routes multiplied and commercial wealth increased. It was shaped by the aristocratic taste for elegance, ornamental variety, and decorative splendor. The beautifully observed natural detail of Gothic art was often incorporated into more realistic settings, but was still represented within an overall decorative scheme. Nurtured in its main centers of Paris and Burgundy – where the grace and delicacy of French manuscript illustration fused with the imagery and style of both Sienese and Flemish painting – the fashionable courtly style also had a persuasive influence in northern Italy.

DECORATIVE TAPESTRY
International Gothic, with its ornamental style, was especially suited to the decorative nature of tapestry. The Devonshire Hunting Tapestries (detail of *The Bear and Boar Hunt*, c.1430–35, above) are some of the few surviving early 15th-century examples.

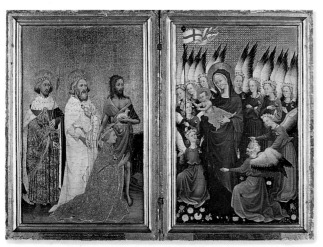

THE WILTON DIPTYCH
c.1395; each wing: 21 x 14½ in (53 x 37 cm); tempera on panel
This diptych (p. 25), which may have been King Richard II's private altarpiece, shows him being presented to the Virgin and Child by King Edmund, King Edward the Confessor, and St. John the Baptist – the angels wear the white hart of King Richard's livery. The grace of the figures and delicate detail are typical of the new style.

Interior of the diptych

Exterior of the diptych

The right wing shows the white hart of Richard II

The arms of Edward the Confessor are impaled on King Richard II's royal coat of arms

APRIL (FROM "LES TRES RICHES HEURES DU DUC DE BERRY")
The Limbourg brothers (Pol, Herman, and Jean) worked for the Duke of Berry, who was one of the greatest collectors of illuminated books and owned more than 150 sumptuous manuscripts. They decorated a Book of Hours (a religious book offering prayers and meditations appropriate to each hour, day, or month) for him, the famous *Très Riches Heures*. This full-page illustration from the *Très Riches Heures* is a perfect example of International Gothic elegance, showing sinuous figures clothed in rich draperies, in a deep naturalistic landscape.

Adoration of the Magi

GENTILE DA FABRIANO *1423;*
ft 10 in x 9 ft 3 in (3.00 x 2.82 m); tempera on panel

This flamboyant work was painted by the northern Italian artist Gentile da Fabriano (c.1370–1427) for one of the wealthiest citizens in Florence, Palla Strozzi. Gentile had been employed by the Venetian government and the princely courts of northern Italy: Strozzi now expected him to use his courtly style to display his own wealth and rank. The altarpiece was made for the Sacristy of Santa Trinità, the chapel where the clergy dressed in their gorgeous ceremonial attire. The ornate frame is matched by the splendor of the Magi (the Three Kings) and their retinue, who wind though the hills to pay homage to the new-born Christ. Their finery – and the sheer abundance of natural detail – vividly evoke the joyous nature of the occasion.

Tiny painted panels in the side of the frame are filled with fruits and flowers

EXPERIMENTS WITH LIGHT
This scene, from the predella panel of Gentile's *Adoration of the Magi*, may show the journey of Mary, Joseph, and the child Christ from Bethelehem to Jerusalem (although it is often described as representing the flight into Egypt). Here, Gentile has abandoned the conventional gold background (seen in the sky of the main panel) and has created an atmospheric landscape with a real blue sky. The soft, natural light emanating from the gilded sun marks the beginning of a new phase of naturalism in Italian art. Light illuminates the distant buildings, gentle hills, and the fruit and foliage.

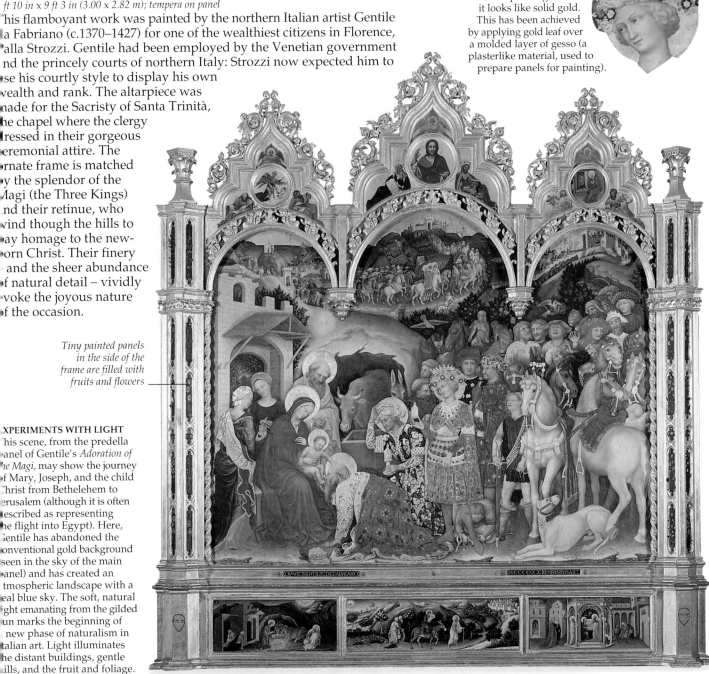

The Brancacci Chapel

Masaccio (1401–28) was the first great Italian painter of the Early Renaissance. Building on the legacy of Giotto (pp. 8–9) and embracing the innovations of his Florentine contemporaries – Donatello's expressive sculpture (p. 15) and Brunelleschi's perspective system (pp. 28–29) – he developed a sober, monumental style of profound naturalism. Christened Tommaso, he was nicknamed Masaccio ("clumsy Tom") because of his lack of worldliness and his slovenly appearance. His art, too, is plain and unadorned, showing little interest in the intricate detail of the International Gothic style and concentrating instead on the physical and spiritual bulk of his figures. Masaccio's most famous work is in Florence: an unforgettable fresco cycle in the Brancacci Chapel, Santa Maria del Carmine, executed alongside works by his collaborator, Masolino di Panicale (active 1423–47).

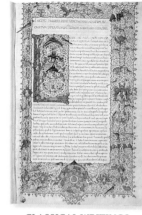

CLASSICAL WRITINGS
The translation of Pliny's *Natural History* (1st century A.D.) in 147... enhanced Masaccio's reputation... it describes the realism of ancient paintings in terms that clearly applied to Masaccio's work.

THE RAISING OF TABITHA
Masolino di Panicale; c.1425;
7 ft 5 in x 19 ft 7 in (2.25 x 5.98 m); fresco
The Brancacci Chapel frescoes were commissioned by the wealthy merchant and diplomat Felice Brancacci in 1423, and work began the following year. In 1428, the fresco cycle was left unfinished, to be completed in 1481–82 by Filippino Lippi. Masolino's elegant style, with its flamboyant use of the new perspective system, has suffered by comparison with the weighty naturalism of Masaccio. In this fresco, the two biblical episodes of the Healing of the Cripple (on the left) and the Raising of Tabitha (on the right) appear within a contemporary Florentine setting. The cobblestones, which become smaller the farther away they appear, lead the eye into a townscape filled with detail.

The Tribute Money

MASACCIO *c.1425; 7 ft 5 in x 19 ft 7 in (2.25 x 5.98 m); fresco*
Masaccio and Masolino seem to have worked together from the beginning, dividing the spaces equally between them. The two most famous scenes, *The Raising of Tabitha* (above right) and *The Tribute Money* (right), are at the same level on facing walls. Both are painted from the same viewpoint, with the ground sloping upward; we feel that we can enter the scenes. Masaccio's "modernity" can be seen in the intensity and gravity of the poses and facial expressions; in the way the viewer's attention is focused by the perspective construction (all the receding lines of the architecture lead to Christ's head); and in the unifying light, which gives airiness to the landscape and substance to the realistically draped figures.

SCULPTURAL INSPIRATION

Masaccio was influenced by the sculpture of Giovanni Pisano (active c.1265–1314), son of the famous Pisan sculptor Nicola Pisano (active c.1258–78). The Pisani revived the heroic forms of classical sculpture, and also inspired Giotto's figure style. The head of Adam in Masaccio's *Expulsion* (detail, below left) was probably inspired by Giovanni's vivid portrayal of the damned on the pulpit of Pisa Cathedral (1302–10; left).

Pisano's figure borrows its pose from the familiar ancient type known as the "modest Venus"

The weight of the figure is taken on one leg, following the example of antique statues (p. 48)

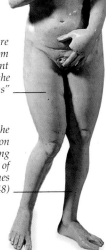

EVE'S ANCESTOR
The figure of Eve in Masaccio's *Expulsion* (right) is similar to Giovanni Pisano's figure of Temperance on the pulpit of Pisa Cathedral – which is itself based on a classical figure type.

SOULS IN TORMENT
Like Giotto, Masaccio uses the physical posture of his figures to reveal the emotions of their souls. Eve's abandoned suffering is expressed through the pitiful angle of her head, Adam's more private torment through the way he stoops in shame, shading his face with his hands. As he leans forward, so she throws her head back, her mouth open in a cry of anguish.

THE EXPULSION
Masaccio; c.1427; 82 x 34¾ in (208 x 88 cm); fresco
Masaccio's harrowing scene of the expulsion of Adam and Eve from the Garden of Eden shows the expressive force and directness of his style. An angel drives the sinners into the harsh, barren world, where the light mercilessly exposes their guilt and despair. Masaccio's composition is beautifully balanced within the narrow format. The forward movement, dictated by the gesture of the angel, is firmly anchored by the strong vertical running from the heads of Adam and Eve to their heels. The muscular tension of Adam's body, and the fluidity of Eve's, were inspired by a contemporary relief.

THE TEMPTATION
Masolino di Panicale; c.1425; 82 x 34¾ in (208 x 88 cm); fresco
Masolino's *Temptation*, in which Eve is tempted by the devil in the guise of a serpent, faces Masaccio's *Expulsion* across the entrance to the Brancacci Chapel. The contrast between the two couples – Masolino's is graceful and courtly, Masaccio's is heavy, contorted, and emotionally charged – reveals the differing artistic visions of the two painters. The figures of Masaccio are stark, but their rounded forms fill the space they stand in; they seem to embody the essence of humanity, while Masolino's have an air of detachment.

Flemish naturalism

In the North, the spirit of Flemish art was transformed by the dramatic naturalism and monumental style of sculpture from Burgundy (p. 14). The Tournai master Robert Campin (c.1375–1444) was the first to flesh out his holy figures and place them in "real," everyday interiors, filled with sacred symbols. The famous Bruges artist Jan van Eyck (active 1422–41) rendered the minute detail of such settings with breathtaking realism, his revolutionary oil technique allowing him to create subtle effects of light, space, and texture. The spiritual essence of a scene was displayed with similar technical virtuosity by Rogier van der Weyden (c.1339–1464). His international renown was exceeded only by that of Hugo van der Goes (active 1467–82), who united van Eyck's naturalism with penetrating studies of humanity.

A MAN IN A TURBAN
Jan van Eyck; 1433; 13 x 10¼ in (33.3 x 25.8 cm); oil on panel
This picture, which is still in its original frame, is often identified as a self-portrait of van Eyck. The frame is inscribed with his modest motto, "As I can," at the top (this may be a pun on his name: "As Eyck can"), and "Jan van Eyck made me on 21 October 1433" along the bottom. The astonishing sense of the sitter's presence is created through contrasts of light and shadow: the face (complete with stubble) seems to project out of the frame, emerging dramatically from the dark background.

THE ARNOLFINI MARRIAGE
Jan van Eyck; 1434; 32¼ x 23½ in (81.8 x 59.7 cm); oil on panel
This double portrait shows van Eyck's mastery of natural light effects, from the clear daylight filtering through the window to the convex mirror on the back wall, which reveals light streaming through a doorway (detail, below). The picture is thought to mark the marriage of an Italian merchant, Giovanni Arnolfini (living in Bruges), to Giovanna Cenami. Van Eyck seems to have invested ordinary items with deeper meanings: the chair, for instance, is carved with the figure of St. Margaret, the patron saint of childbirth.

In medieval symbolism, a lighted candle represents God

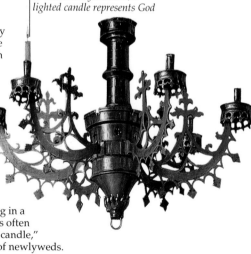

SYMBOLIC LIGHT
The brass chandelier (detail, right) reveals not only the delicacy of van Eyck's light effects, but also a lone candle burning in a room filled with daylight. It is often interpreted as the "marriage candle," traditionally lit in the home of newlyweds.

Detail of the slashed sleeve, from van Eyck's *The Arnolfini Marriage*

PAINTING IN OIL
These details show the intricate effects that can be achieved using oil paint (colors blended in a medium of oil, such as linseed or walnut). Van Eyck refined the technique, using the transparency of certain oil colors to build deep, jewel-like tones and blending the slow-drying paint with his fingertips.

Detail of brocade underskirt, from van der Weyden's *The Magdalen Reading* (above right)

MIRROR IMAGE
This detail shows how the mirror frame is decorated with scenes from Christ's Passion (his suffering and Crucifixion) and Resurrection. The mirror itself reflects two more figures – visitors, or even marriage witnesses. The artist's inscription above – "Jan van Eyck was here, 1434" – suggests that he may be one of them!

THE MAGDALEN READING

Rogier van der Weyden; c.1445; 24¼ x 21½ in (61.6 x 54.6 cm); oil on panel
This fragment from an altarpiece shows Mary Magdalen, one of the holy women, reading in an ordinary room. Van der Weyden has included selective details, such as the delicate carvings of the wooden cupboard and the glinting tacks in the floorboards. The subtle handling of light, however, which illuminates the whites of Mary Magdalen's headdress and draped Bible, focuses the viewer's gaze on her demure figure.

SYMBOLS OF REPENTANCE

Mary Magdalen is shown by her "attribute" of the ointment jar, an object that is always associated with her. The jar (detail, above) contains costly myrrh, which she used to anoint Christ. She reads from a precious illuminated Bible (right) that matches her rich attire and symbolizes her new life of holy works. Once a courtesan, she now personifies repentance – inviting sinners to restore themselves by her example.

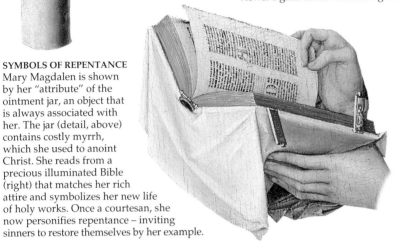

ADORATION OF THE SHEPHERDS (PORTINARI ALTARPIECE)

Hugo van der Goes; c.1476–78; 8 ft 3 in x 19 ft 2 in (2.53 x 5.86 m); oil on panel
The huge *Portinari Altarpiece*, by the Ghent master Hugo van der Goes, was commissioned by the Medici representative in Bruges, Tommaso Portinari, for his chapel in Sant'Egidio, Florence. Its arrival in 1483 caused a great stir among Italian artists. The central panel depicts the Nativity and the adoration of the shepherds, while the wings include portraits of the Portinari family and their patron saints. The extreme realism of the aged male saints and coarse-featured shepherds is matched by the naturalism of the landscape.

PORTRAITS FROM LIFE

The portraits of the Portinari children have been used to date the altarpiece. They and their mother were painted from life, directly onto the wings (c.1477–78). But it seems that Tommaso's head was painted on a separate surface before the wings were started (because he was leaving for Italy), and later glued into place.

MEANING IN THE FLOWERS

The natural still life in the foreground of the Nativity scene is symbolic: the scarlet lily, for instance, represents the red blood of Christ; the purple columbines symbolize the sorrows of the Virgin; and the sheaf of grain refers to Christ's birthplace, Bethlehem (Hebrew: "house of bread").

The artist's craft

THE ARTIST'S ROLE in the Renaissance was much more varied than that of artists today. Artists learned their craft in a busy workshop, run by a master who obtained the commissions they worked on. They ground colors, prepared wooden panels for painting, gilded in gold leaf, and mastered a range of techniques. The work undertaken ranged from altarpieces and grand murals in churches, town halls, and palaces, to small images for prayer, civic portraits (often sent as diplomatic gifts), painted furniture, festival decorations, book covers, and stage sets. Style and subject matter were often dictated by the function of a picture, as well as the surroundings in which it was to be seen.

THE CRAFTSMAN'S HANDBOOK
Cennino Cennini's *The Craftsman's Handbook* (c.1400) provides a vivid account of early Italian fresco and egg tempera techniques (p. 63). Egg tempera was the most popular medium for 15th-century Italian panel paintings.

ST. LUKE PAINTING THE VIRGIN AND CHILD
Follower of Quinten Massys; 1510–30;
44¾ x 13¾ in (113.7 x 34.9 cm); oil on panel
Pictures of artists at this time usually depict St. Luke, the patron saint of painters. They also give an idea of the tools and materials used by Renaissance artists. This Flemish panel shows the saint, who is identified by his symbol of the ox, painting a portrait of the Virgin. The fine brushes and the stick, which he uses to steady his hand, reveal the painstaking nature of his technique.

CONTRACTS
For most major commissions, the patron – who paid for a work of art – detailed requirements in a contractual agreement. This contract, for an altarpiece of 1453 by the artist Enguerrand Quarton, insists that the finest pigments be used, and specifies the subject matter and medium.

PAINT SUPPLIERS
The apothecaries, whose medicinal skill is shown in this Latin manuscript illustration, were closely identified with painters (in Florence, they belonged to the same guild – the Guild of St. Luke – along with the spice merchants and doctors). They were one of the main suppliers of pigments – colors in powdered form, from natural earths, minerals, plants, or animal materials – used by artists. Religious orders often supplied the most costly colors of ultramarine blue and vermilion red.

PAINTING SUPPORTS
Most Renaissance artists worked on wooden panels. These were made from poplar, oak, silver fir, and other suitable woods: this one, part of the reverse of a painting of St. Paul, is made of white poplar, which was the preferred support in Italy. After 1450, canvas, which had been used largely for temporary festival decorations and theatrical scenery, became more common. In 16th-century Venice (pp. 44–45), canvas was used for large-scale works because it could be rolled up and transported easily. It also resisted the city's damp conditions better than fresco or panel.

The Medici emblem of three feathers in a ring appears on the parapet in the center of the painting

The Virgin's bedstead is decorated with inlaid wood designs

THE BIRTH OF ST. JOHN THE BAPTIST
Giovanni di Paolo; c.1427; 12 x 14¼ in (30.8 x 36.4 cm); tempera on panel
Religious images were the mainstay of the artist's workshop: they ranged from full-blown altarpieces (which were placed on church or chapel altars) to small paintings of the Virgin and Child, designed for private devotion in the home. This panel, by the Sienese painter Giovanni di Paolo (active 1425–83), is one of five scenes from the life of St. John the Baptist, which once formed the predella of an altarpiece. It shows St. Elizabeth lying exhausted in bed after giving birth to St. John the Baptist. The head and foot of the bed are decorated with painted panels, as was the custom in Giovanni di Paolo's day (see above).

THE ANNUNCIATION
Fra Filippo Lippi; c.1448; 27 x 60 in (68.6 x 152.4 cm); tempera on panel
This panel by Fra Filippo Lippi (c.1406–69), with its sweet domestic setting, was designed for the *camera* – an intimate chamber that was used as both drawing room and bedroom. It is one of two half-moon-shaped pictures by Lippi, which were probably placed above beds in the Medici Palace. Panels of inlaid wood (Italian: *intarsie*) were also popular in such rooms, as were beautiful fabrics and wall hangings. In wealthy households, Netherlandish tapestries, which were more costly than paintings, were displayed most prominently; in *The Annunciation*, the "carpet" of foliage and flowers deliberately imitates tapestry patterns.

WEDDING CHEST
A number of the narrow, horizontal Italian paintings that survive, such as Uccello's *Hunt* (p. 28), once decorated wedding chests (Italian: *cassoni*) or their back panels (Italian: *spalliere*). The chests often sported stirring narratives illustrating manly virtues – and matching images of female virtues. This *cassone* is one of a pair created for a society wedding of 1472, and still has its *spalliera* intact.

THE YOUTHFUL DAVID
Andrea del Castagno; c.1450; 45½ x 30¼ in (115.6 x 76.9 cm); oil on leather, on panel
Painters had to work on all types of commissions, including decorations for festivals and pageants. The great Florentine master Andrea del Castagno (c.1419–57) painted this leather shield, which was probably carried in jousts. Appropriately, the winner of the battle, David, stands over the slain Goliath.

Images of devotion

DURING THE RENAISSANCE, there was a huge demand for religious images. The number of altarpieces increased as they were commissioned by orders of monks and friars, guilds, the confraternities (lay associations devoted to religious cults or works of charity), and wealthy citizens, while small, ready-made pictures were bought by pious individuals. In Italy, whole chapels were often frescoed with cycles illustrating stories from the Bible (pp. 8–9; pp. 18–19). In the North, stained glass, and the great portal sculptures of figures and reliefs around church doorways, served a similar purpose. Much of the imagery was dominated by the lives of the saints – their martyrdom had inspired the early Church – and the cult of the Virgin. Altarpieces depicting the crucified Christ were also common, providing an appropriate backdrop to the ritual celebration of Mass.

HOLY RELICS
Martyred saints were often adopted as patrons. Churches were named after their patron saint, and all altars contained relics (believed to be pieces of the saint's body or clothing), which were objects of veneration. This reliquary from San Domenico's in Bologna, Italy, contains St. Dominic's skull.

THE DEPOSITION
Fra Angelico; c.1440–45; 108¼ x 112¼ in (275 x 285 cm); tempera on panel
The Italian painter Fra Angelico (1387–1455) was a Dominican friar, and placed his art at the service of his order. This altarpiece, painted for the Strozzi family chapel in the Florentine Church of Santa Trinità, is radiantly colored to shine in the chapel's gloom.

PREACHING SERMONS
Popular preachers like Fra Roberto Caracciolo (shown in this Florentine woodcut of 1491) made the teachings of the Church accessible to an illiterate public. Fra Roberto infused holy stories with drama, explained their significance, and indicated the appropriate emotional response. The gestures and actions, made recognizable by preachers, were used in similar ways by painters to provoke pious emotions.

THE VIRGIN AND CHILD WITH SAINTS FRANCIS AND SEBASTIAN
Carlo Crivelli; 1491; 69 x 59½ in (175.3 x 151.1 cm); oil on panel
This altarpiece, by the Venetian painter Carlo Crivelli (active 1457–93), was painted for a Franciscan church. It shows St. Francis (on the left) and St. Sebastian – who is pierced with the arrows of his martyrdom – flanking the Virgin and Child. Crivelli's altarpiece was commissioned by the widow Oradea – and her portrait is included. She is the tiny figure peeping out from behind St. Francis's leg (detail, right). Such portraits of the benefactor ("donor" portraits), however, were often shown the same size as the holy figures (p. 21).

GESTURES
These two details from Fra Angelico's altarpiece illustrate how gestures are used to tell a story and reveal particular emotions. One man crosses his hands in an expression of humility (above right). The kneeling foreground figure (right) commends the viewer to Christ's mercy, inviting him or her to pay similar homage to Christ. His right hand is held to his chest in a gesture of reverence.

The Deposition
ROGIER VAN DER WEYDEN
c.1435; 86½ x 103 in (220 x 262 cm); oil on panel

Van der Weyden emphasized the spiritual elements of the scenes he painted: this moving episode shows Christ being lowered from the cross by Nicodemus (a secret disciple) and Joseph of Arimathea. The Virgin, in a faint, is supported by St. John the Evangelist, whose rhythmic, stooping posture is mirrored by that of the grief-stricken Mary Magdalen opposite. The figures are compressed into a shallow space, much like the sculpted wooden shrines (below) that decorated Gothic churches.

This was once the central panel of a triptych (see below)

MUTUAL SUFFERING
The Virgin's pale hand, limp with grief, is movingly juxtaposed with the mutilated hand of her crucified Son.

ARCHERS' BOWS
Tiny crossbows in the tracery refer to the Archers' Guild, which commissioned the altarpiece.

ST. WOLFGANG ALTARPIECE
The Austrian sculptor and painter Michael Pacher (active 1462–98) produced elaborate carved, painted, and gilded altarpieces. This massive work (1471–81) has a sculpted, gilded shrine at its center; is topped with pinnacles and painted figures; and is closed with painted wings – as is the predella panel. Decorated with scenes from the *Life of the Virgin* and the *Legend of St. Wolfgang*, it is shown here in the Church of St. Wolfgang, near Salzburg. Pacher himself supervised its installation there, as his contract with his patron, the Abbot of Mondsee, had specified.

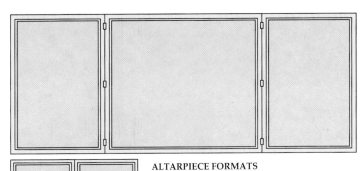

ALTARPIECE FORMATS
Altarpieces take various forms: the diptych (left) has two hinged panels that close like a book; a triptych (above), three panels – the wings close; and a polyptych, several panels (such as Duccio's *Maestà*, p. 10). There is also the single rectangular panel, the *"pala d'altare,"* an innovation of the Italian Renaissance.

Classical inspiration

THE 15TH-CENTURY ENTHUSIASM for the remains of ancient Rome followed in the wake of the rediscovery of classical manuscripts in the Middle Ages. Mythological and classical themes gained in popularity and artists studied the monuments and sculptures that surrounded them. A growing awareness of Italy's cultural origins was also stimulated by the continual unearthing of statues and artifacts. The ancient reliefs, which had inspired Gothic artists with their natural forms, became a treasure trove of dramatic poses and stylistic ideas. While artists like Donatello and Andrea del Verrocchio (1435–88) revived classical types, from the colossal equestrian monument to the small bronze statuette, the northern Italian master Andrea Mantegna (1431–1506) combined his wide interests in archaeology (which included the recording of classical inscriptions) with artistic invention.

CHRIST BEFORE PILATE
Jacopo Bellini (1400–70/1), the father of Giovanni (pp. 34–35), used antique motifs in a free and imaginative manner. This page from his volume of drawings reflects the fashion for setting New Testament subjects in their Roman context: here, Christ is brought to trial before Pontius Pilate beneath a triumphal arch (see left).

The equestrian monument embodies the Roman ideal of public virtue

THE ARCH OF TITUS
The triumphal Arch of Titus (c.81 A.D.) stands in the Forum in Rome. The reliefs on such arches, which commemorated imperial processions and battles, were avidly copied by artists and antiquarians. The arches themselves often appear in fanciful guise in the backgrounds of paintings.

CLASSICAL TRANSLATIONS
The humanist scholar Lionardo Bruni was a driving force behind the translation of many classical Greek works into Latin in the 15th century. This manuscript page begins his account of the ancient Punic War (in which the Romans defeated the Carthaginians), based on the work of the Greek Polybius. It was made for the library of the Gonzaga family in Mantua and is adorned with their crest and arms of 1433.

GATTAMELATA
Donatello; 1445–53; height:
12 ft 2 in (3.70 m); bronze
Donatello's huge equestrian portrait of the mercenary captain Gattamelata revives one of the grandest and most technically ambitious forms of ancient sculpture – the monumental equestrian bronze. It emulates the antique equestrian statue of Marcus Aurelius in Rome (late 2nd century A.D.), which had survived because it was thought to show the Christian emperor Constantine. Donatello's horse is directly adapted from one of the four ancient gilded horses on the facade of San Marco in Venice.

THE INTRODUCTION OF THE CULT OF CYBELE AT ROME ("THE TRIUMPH OF SCIPIO")
Andrea Mantegna; 1505–6;
29 x 105½ in (73.7 x 268 cm); monochrome on canvas
This episode from the Punic Wars shows the Romans bearing the goddess Cybele in the form of a stone, and her bust. Prophecies had decreed that the Carthaginians would only be expelled from Italy if the goddess was carried from Asia Minor to Rome and received by the city's worthiest man; Scipio Nasica was chosen. Mantegna painted the scene (commissioned by the Cornaros, who claimed to be descendants of the Scipios) to look like a Roman cameo. The figures – some of which are based on actual Roman reliefs and statues – appear against an exquisite simulated marble background.

HERCULES AND ANTAEUS
Antonio del Pollaiuolo; c.1470s; height: 18 in (45.7 cm); bronze

This small-scale bronze of wrestling figures by the Florentine artist Antonio del Pollaiuolo (active 1457–98) imitates antique examples. In his portrayal of Hercules and Antaeus in violent conflict, Pollaiuolo was one of the first to present a mythological subject in three dimensions. It is so dramatically styled and anatomically detailed that it almost demands to be rotated so that its multiple viewpoints can be admired. The idea of displaying figures from contrasting viewpoints was also practiced by Pollaiuolo in his paintings to show that two-dimensional works could equal sculpture in their realism.

Antaeus's agonized expression and taut arm show the body at breaking point

Flying limbs animate the surrounding space

Hercules's calves ripple with straining muscles

‑EATH OF ORPHEUS (AFTER MANTEGNA)
‑lthough the Northern interest in antiquity ‑as initially based in classical writings, woodcuts ‑f Italian works in the antique style were copied ‑ 15th-century workshops. Similarly, Dürer ‑p. 40–41) looked to Italian artists rather than ‑irectly to the antique. His fascination with Italy's ‑rtistic heritage was fostered by his friendship with ‑e Nuremberg humanist Willibald Pirckheimer. ‑his, together with his determination to master ‑e art of engraving, led Dürer to make drawings ‑fter famous mythological prints by Mantegna. ‑ürer's pen drawing of 1494, after a lost Mantegna ‑ngraving, shows the poet Orpheus being clubbed ‑ death by the women of Thrace, and reflects ‑ürer's own vigorous response to the scene.

PUTTO AND DOLPHIN
Andrea del Verrocchio; c.1470s; 26½ in (67 cm); bronze

This winged infant was made for the center of a fountain at the Medici country villa of Careggi, a place for leisure and intellectual pursuits. Its light-hearted charm reflects the relaxed atmosphere that was associated with country villas of classical times.

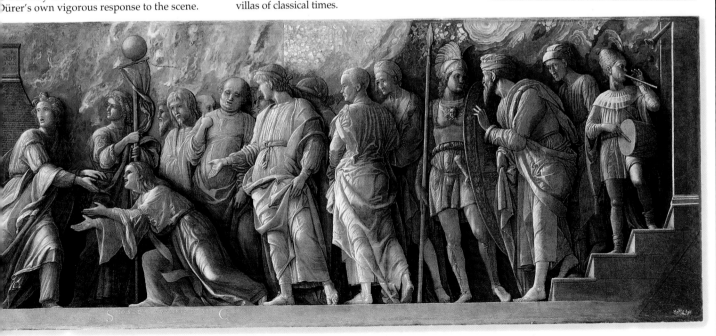

The "invention" of perspective

Lᴉɴᴇᴀʀ ᴘᴇʀsᴘᴇᴄᴛᴉᴠᴇ – a mathematical system
for representing three-dimensional space on a
flat surface – was devised in Florence in the early
15th century. Brunelleschi (p. 12) demonstrated its
principles, but a fellow architect and writer, Leon
Battista Alberti (1404–72), was the first to formulate
rules that the artist could follow. In Alberti's system,
the picture surface is imagined as an "open window" through which
a painted world is seen. He showed how a perspective "checkerboard
pavement" (like a squared floor) is created within the picture space
– in which the receding parallel lines (the orthogonals) represent
visual rays connecting the spectator's eye to a spot in the distance.
This spot, on which all the rays converge, is known as the "vanishing
point," and is positioned directly opposite the spectator's viewpoint.
The single viewpoint meant that the artist could now control
and focus the way the spectator looked at his picture.

ETIENNE CHEVALIER WITH ST. STEPHE
Jean Fouquet; c.1450; 36½ x 33¾
(93 x 86 cm); oil on pa
In Northern painting, perspective w
judged by eye, rather than being dictate
by theoretical rules. Jean Fouquet (c.142
c.1481), France's leading painter ar
illuminator, visited Italy and becan
fascinated with the construction
spatial settings. In this panel, I
uses his favored diagonal form
with the diminishing squares of t
"checkerboard" floor tiles (a comm
device) and the spacing between t
architectural columns providing t
main perspective clues, along wi
the wonderful manipulation of ligl

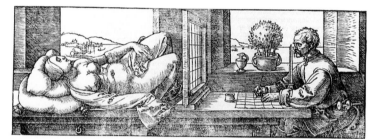

ALBERTI'S DEVICES
As a perspective aid, Alberti
devised his grid or "veil" – a
transparent material divided
into squares by colored threads
and stretched over a frame. This
device, illustrated in this treatise
by Dürer (1525), was placed
between "the eye and the object
to be represented" so that the
object could be drawn to scale.

THE HUNT IN THE FOREST
Paolo Uccello; 1460s;
28¾ x 69¾ in (73 x 177 cm);
tempera and oil on panel
The Florentine artist Paolo
Uccello (1397–1475) was so
enamored with the new
"science" of perspective that,
according to Vasari, he used
to stay up all night searching
for vanishing points. This
obsession can be seen in his
paintings, which playfully
experiment with all manner
of objects that lead the eye
back into space. Here, horses
charge toward an off-center
vanishing point, with carefully
placed logs pointing the way.

UCCELLO'S FRAMEWORK
This perspective analysis of Uccello's *Hunt* shows
the importance of the "horizon line" in perspectival
construction. This horizontal line, drawn across the
painting at the vanishing point, represents both the
viewer's eye level and the far distance. It creates the
sense of a three-dimensional space by making us
assume that the forest floor (which slopes upward) is
flat. We imagine the tiny running figures to be roughly
the same height as we are, because if one of the figures
was positioned at the very front of the picture, his
eye level would be on the horizon line, like ours. The
orthogonals of the "pavement" are marked by the bases
of the standing tree trunks, which lead our eye to the
vanishing point near a far tree (encircled by hounds).

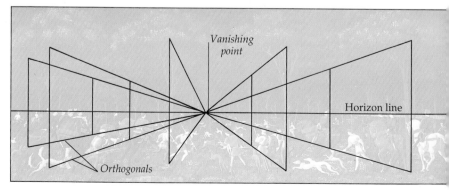

Vanishing point

Horizon line

Orthogonals

Adoration of the Kings
BRAMANTINO
*c.1498; 22½ x 21¼ in
(56.8 x 55 cm); oil on panel*

The Milanese painter
and architect Bramantino
(c.1465–1530), a pupil of
Bramante (p. 51), wrote
a treatise on perspective
(now lost) and had an
unusually complete grasp
of perspective method.
His *Adoration of the Kings*
gives us a remarkable
insight into the way
Alberti's system worked
in practice, because the
numerous constructional
lines – of the receding
perspective grid – are
actually ruled and incised
in the preparatory gesso
(see artwork, below left).
Bramantino used this
perspective framework
to scale his figures and
architecture and position
them correctly in space,
but he also took pains
to disguise the textbook
rigidity of the construction.

BRAMANTINO'S PERSPECTIVE PAVEMENT
Bramantino divided the base
of his picture into six equal
units, incising orthogonals
from these points to a central
vanishing point just below the
Virgin's knee. Lines were also
incised from the top corners
down to this vanishing point.
Bramantino then continued the
horizon line – drawn through
the vanishing point – out to
the left of the picture space (on
a separate work surface), to a
point representing the chosen
viewing distance. From here,
Bramantino drew lines to the
units at the base of the picture.
Where these lines intersected
the left edge, Bramantino made
a series of marks, from which
he incised the horizontal lines
of his pavement. This framework was, however, used
imaginatively: three containers
placed in the foreground lead
the eye into the distance subtly.

Vanishing point

Horizon line

Orthogonals

*Two extra
steps, cloaked
in shadow in
the painting,
rise behind the
Virgin's seat*

FIGURES ON THE DAIS
The grid units – the "tiles" of the perspective
pavement – provide a ground plan for all the
objects in the painting. This plan is so precise
that computer graphics can "erect" the stepped
dais, and the main figures positioned upon it,
three-dimensionally. It can even show the dais
from a side viewpoint (above). This suggests
that Bramantino may have employed a three-
dimensional model with movable figures
when working out details such as the lighting.

Harmony and beauty

AN ANCIENT IDEAL of beauty, based on mathematical and musical notions of harmony and proportion, was revived in Italian Renaissance circles. The theorist and architect Alberti explained in *De Re Aedificatoria*, his 1485 treatise on architecture, that "Everything that Nature produces is regulated by the law of harmony, and her chief concern is that everything should be perfect. Without harmony this could hardly be achieved, for the critical sympathy of the parts would be lost." This perfect harmony, its balance destroyed if anything is added or subtracted, can be created by the artist or architect through a careful arrangement of component parts. The flawless logic of mathematics will ensure that the parts of a painting or building are proportionally related to the whole – thus forming the beauty of ideal proportion. The human body itself, the "noblest living form," was regarded as a model for God's universe; using the measure of the body, the artist could construct the wider world.

ROMAN LETTERING
One of the most enduring legacies of the Renaissance fascination with proportion the geometrical construction of Roman lettering. Dürer introduced this "secret" to the North. His method (left outlined in his treatise *On the Just Shaping of Letters*, is taken from a Venetian handbook.

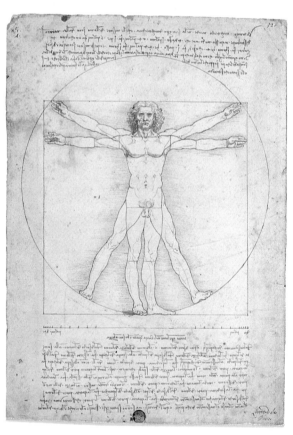

MAN, THE MEASURE OF ALL THINGS
Leonardo's famous drawing, *Vitruvian Man* (c.1487), illustrates a classical formula devised by Vitruvius. It is simply explained by the mathematician Luca Pacioli, who often worked with Leonardo: "Having considered the right arrangement of the human body, the ancients proportioned all their work, particularly the temples, in accordance with it. In the human body they discovered the two main figures without which it is impossible to achieve anything, namely the perfect circle and the square." Spread-eagled, the man fits into a circle; with feet together and arms outstretched, he fits into a square.

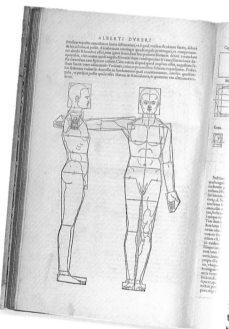

BUILDING PROPORTIONS
Alberti's facade for the Rucellai Palace in Florence (1455–58) consists of three stories of equal height, divided by pilasters (the fla upright pillars) that suppor entablatures (the horizonta elements). The pilasters are topped with capitals, which are as wide as the central entablatures are tall.

ON HUMAN PROPORTION
Dürer was inspired by his reading of a treatise by the Roman archite Vitruvius (1st century B.C.), and studies of proportion by Leonardo Vinci (far left; pp. 36–37), to write h own work on the subject (1528; left He divided figures of different heig into sections, and carefully calculate their measurements as fractions of t total length – as "parts" of the "whol

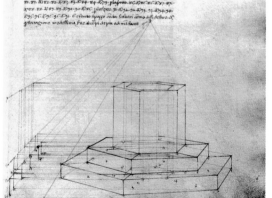

PERSPECTIVE ARRANGIN
This drawing of a *Wellhead* is from a perspective treatis by Piero della Francesca (c.1415/20–92), the great painter and mathematical theorist. Pacioli (Piero's pupil) said that "nine out ten words" of this treatise were, in fact, on proportio the art of arranging things. Here, Piero shows how a three-dimensional object can be constructed from a plan and logically positioned in space. The proportions are mathematically calculated with the utmost precision.

The Baptism of Christ

PIERO DELLA FRANCESCA

1450s; 65¾ x 45¾ in (167 x 116 cm); tempera on panel

The monumental grandeur and apparent simplicity of this altarpiece derives partly from the fact that it uses exact proportional arithmetic and is constructed around pure geometrical shapes (below). Piero valued "the placing of profiles and contours in their proper places in proportion" in an image. He places the figure of Christ, thought to be the most perfect of "human" forms, at the very center of the work, making him half as tall as the panel is high.

MATHEMATICAL DIVISIONS

Piero's composition is divided into halves (passing through the figure and face of Christ) and thirds (on which the tree, Christ, and St. John the Baptist are placed); even the relationship between the height of the panel and its width is in a ratio of about 3:2. Two circles, one with the dove of the Holy Spirit at its center, the other with the tips of Christ's fingers, make mathematical and symbolic sense of this arrangement.

THE HARMONIC SCALE

This woodcut of 1480 shows the theory of Western musical harmony developed by the mathematician Pythagoras (6th century B.C.). The musical scale was divided into harmonic intervals, which were expressed through numbers. Its sequence – 6, 8, 9, 12 – and its harmonic proportions (the interval between 6 and 12 is an octave, between 8 and 9 a tone) were adapted by some painters and architects.

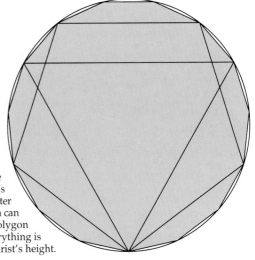

EUCLIDIAN GEOMETRY

It is thought that Piero used Euclid's ancient formula for constructing a 15-sided polygon as the mathematical basis for *The Baptism of Christ* (which would be in the position of the lower circle, above right). The wings of the dove are arranged along the baseline of the upside-down equilateral triangle, with Christ's right foot at its downward point. From the center of this, a circle, pentagon, and, finally, a polygon can be generated. The length of each side of the polygon is the unit of measurement around which everything is constructed: it is exactly one-third of Christ's height.

Botticelli and mythology

THE CELEBRATED *Primavera* ("Spring") by Sandro Botticelli (1445–1510), a large imaginary scene depicting figures from ancient mythology, represented a new type of picture, prized in cultured Renaissance circles. It is the painted equivalent of a lyric poem, invoking the spirit of Venus, goddess of love and springtime, and inviting the viewer to enter her realm of perpetual beauty and abundance. The work was probably commissioned sometime after 1478 for the Medici residence known as the *case vecchie* in Florence, which had been inherited by Lorenzo de' Medici's young wards – it was originally fitted into the wainscoting above a daybed in one of the ground-floor rooms. Vasari mentions that such room decorations were executed with wondrous skill and "poetic invention," and showed jousts, tournaments, festivals, and other spectacles of the time. There is no doubt that this painting is linked to the sumptuous Medici pageants (it may actually commemorate one of them) for which Botticelli painted fabrics and banners. These pageants reflected the rich literary interests of Lorenzo's scholarly circle: drawing on both the vivid classical descriptions of ancient rustic festivals and rites (in Latin verse), and the ornate imagery of Tuscan love poetry and chivalric romance.

ANCIENT INSPIRATION
The group of three figures on the right in the *Primavera* is derived from an ancient myth related in Ovid's *Fasti* (title page, above). In this, the Greek nymph Chloris explains how she became "queen of flowers." As she roamed in spring, Zephyr (the west wind) pursued and raped her, but later married her – making her the goddess of spring, whom the Romans called Flora. Zephyr gave her "a fruitful garden ... filled with noble flowers."

EMBLEM OF THE MEDICI
The Medici emblem of *palle* (Italian: "balls"), from their coat of arms, is subtly alluded to in Botticelli's grove of orange trees, with its mass of rounded golden fruit (right). Other trees have symbolic meanings – the myrtle in the center, for instance, is sacred to Venus.

SEEDS OF FERTILITY
Seed clusters rise around the feet of Mercury, the messenger of the gods. He is shown (on the extreme left) stirring the clouds with his wand, which is adorned with dragonlike snakes (symbols of fertility). His role has perplexed art historians – Botticelli may have included the god because he presided over the seed-dispersing spring winds.

Primavera

SANDRO BOTTICELLI *c.1478;*
80 x 123½ in (203 x 314 cm); tempera on panel
Botticelli's rustic idyll centers on the figure of Venus, who raises her hand in a traditional gesture of welcome. She is attended by her son, Cupid, the god of love, who takes aim with his flaming arrow. Her handmaidens, the Three Graces – goddesses of charm, grace, and beauty – dance at one side. They are shown "with hands interlocked ... smiling and youthful, clad in loosened transparent gowns," just as the ancient author Seneca had described them. He was writing about a lost classical painting in which Mercury stands alongside the Graces. In the Renaissance, Alberti recommended Seneca's description as an imaginative treatment of a subject that painters could emulate.

Mercury · The Three Graces · Cupid · Flora · Zephyr · Venus · Chloris/Flora

FIGURES FROM ANCIENT MYTH

The nine figures in Botticelli's painting originate in ancient Greek and Roman myth. They are almost life-size in scale and are usually identified as above. All are associated with the ancient festivals of springtime, particularly the Floralia (the festivals of Flora). Venus symbolizes the season's fertility, while Mercury and Flora are associated with the month of May.

THE REBIRTH OF CHLORIS

As the goddess of flowers tells of her rustic origins, her mouth, in Ovid's words, "breathes the roses of spring." Botticelli has shown Chloris with flowers streaming from her mouth, as if she is being transformed into Flora at Zephyr's embrace. The figure next to her is often identified as the "reborn" Flora – her cult was in existence in Rome at an early date. She has also been interpreted as the Hour (ancient spirit) of spring.

> *"Ove madonna volge gli occhi belli, senz'altro sol questa novella Flora fa germinar la terra e mandar fora mille vari color di fior novelli."*

> *"Wherever my lady turns her beautiful eyes, with no other sun does this new Flora cause the earth to germinate and to put forth the thousand various colors of the new flowers."*

Lorenzo de' Medici

THE POETRY OF SPRING

The sonnets of Lorenzo (an extract is quoted and translated above) use the season of spring as a metaphor for the fertile power of love – here, his "lady" is identified as Flora, or spring. An acclaimed poet from his circle, Politian (1454–94), draws on the same traditional imagery; the presence of the beloved lady can transform even the most desolate place into a flowering springtime paradise, as seems to be the case in Botticelli's vision.

FESTIVAL COSTUME

Flora's gown may be based on the white dress "painted with roses and flowers and greenery" worn at a Medici tournament of 1475 and commemorated in Politian's verses.

MAY DAY FESTIVALS

This woodcut shows Lorenzo de' Medici at the *Calendimaggio* celebrations in Florence. This popular May Day festival had its origins in the ancient Floralia. Its dancers, like Botticelli's figures, gave welcome to the spring "that makes man fall in love" (Politian).

SCHOLARLY ADVISOR

Artists were sometimes advised by experts – Politian may have shaped Botticelli's "invention." The classical scholar Guarino da Verona, portrayed in this medal, was consulted on details of this painting (right) by Cosimo Tura (active 1451–1495).

AN ALLEGORICAL FIGURE

Cosimo Tura; 1450s; 45¾ x 28 in (116 x 71 cm); oil and tempera on panel
This classical figure, painted for the *studiolo* (a private room for intellectual recreation) of Lionello d'Este of Ferrara, is full of erudite literary symbols that may never be deciphered. It probably shows one of the Nine Muses, who presided over the arts in ancient myth.

The rise of landscape

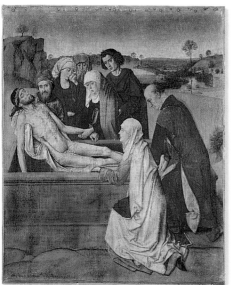

THROUGHOUT THE 15TH CENTURY, there was a growing interest in "landscape" – the depiction of natural scenery in painting. While earlier artists had used a stock formula of rocky outcrops and stylized trees to emphasize the grouping of their figures, painters now filled their backgrounds with a charming variety of narrative detail or created deep vistas to demonstrate their new perspective skills. Instead of the costly gold grounds that were so common in altarpieces, Italian patrons began to specify "landscapes and skies" in their commissions, wishing to acquire something more individually tailored and tasteful. This fashion for decorative landscape detail was imported from the North, where there was a strong tradition of landscape in illuminated manuscripts and tapestries. Northern artists also developed the technical means to create miraculously natural effects of light and distance, using the oil medium to bathe their landscapes in atmosphere.

THE ENTOMBMENT
Dieric Bouts; c.1450–60; 35½ x 29¼ in (90.2 x 74.3 cm); glue size on linen
The Netherlandish painter Dieric Bouts (c.1400–75) used landscape to set a contemplative tone. Here, the figure composition is gently pushed to the left, drawing the eye toward the infinite landscape on the right. The natural background also includes traditional narrative details that are appropriate to the theme: a rocky cliff, symbolic of death, surmounts Christ's lifeless head, while the fertile scenery beyond hints at rebirth and salvation (details, below). Bouts's approach is unusual in that he values the landscape for its own sake, as a place for meditation. His painting technique, in which pigments mixed in glue are absorbed by the linen cloth support, heightens the soft effect (although some of the original depth of color has been lost).

Detail of rocky landscape

Detail of fertile landscape

The Agony in the Garden

GIOVANNI BELLINI *c.1465; 32 x 50 in (81.3 x 127 cm); tempera on panel*
The Venetian artist Giovanni Bellini (c.1435–1516) quietly revolutionized Italian landscape painting. His portrayal of *The Agony in the Garden*, which is closely based on a painting of the same subject by Mantegna, his brother-in-law (above right), is remarkable for its unifying light and all-enveloping atmosphere. Day is breaking, and the rosy light of dawn softens the lines of the gently swelling landscape. Christ kneels in prayer on a cushion of rock, which slopes upward to form a simple altar, while his disciples slumber on the barren ground. As Christ prays, awaiting his arrest, the soldiers are already approaching (led by the traitor Judas) under a departing swathe of dark, rippling cloud. Bellini's landscape lyrically expresses the dawning of Christianity.

VIEW OF THE ARNO VALLEY

Leonardo's landscape studies combine scientific observation with the force of the imagination. This early drawing of the Arno valley in Tuscany represents a real view, dated to a particular day (August 5, 1473). Yet its vast sweep transforms this objective record, unique in its time, into an image of the artist's creative powers. Leonardo had noted how the artist, "as lord and creator," can perceive the world's enormous variety "in a single glance."

THE AGONY IN THE GARDEN

Andrea Mantegna; c.1460; 24¾ x 31½ in (62.9 x 80 cm); tempera on panel

The compressed geological landscape of Mantegna's *Agony* is painted with the precision of a miniaturist. In contrast to Bellini, he has chosen to stress the human agony of Christ's ordeal as he contemplates his imminent Crucifixion. The suffering of Christ is expressed in minute natural details, such as the writhing roots of a fallen tree and the ax marks in its bark (on the right). An awareness of the value placed on illusion by the artists of antiquity probably provided the impetus for Mantegna's inventive realism: the rock seems to shape itself into a shrouded corpse at Christ's knees – a "fantastic invention," worthy of the great classical painters.

ST. JEROME IN A ROCKY LANDSCAPE

Ascribed to Joachim Patenier; 1515; 14 x 13½ in (36.2 x 34.3 cm); oil on panel

The Flemish painter Joachim Patenier (d.1524) was the first artist to specialize in landscapes. This fantastic rocky landscape is surveyed from a high viewpoint – a Northern innovation that had become popular in Italy (as in Leonardo's drawing, above).

The panoramic grandeur of the scenery may also reflect the new conception of the world that followed Columbus's discoveries.

TEMPESTA

Giorgione; c.1505; 32½ x 28¾ in (83 x 73 cm); oil on canvas

With the emergence of the private collector, the actual subject matter of a painting became less defined. Connoisseurs desired more decorative works that would be "pleasing to the eye," would harmonize with their interests (pastoral poetry or music, for instance), and would suit the intimate atmosphere of their private apartments. Small landscape paintings with pastoral or erotic themes first became fashionable in Venice, in the circle of Giorgione (1476/8–1510). His *Tempesta* (Italian: "Storm") is one of the first Italian paintings to be described as a "landscape." Giorgone uses his oil technique, in which light areas emerge from a dark background, to add to the twilight poetry of the scene.

The genius of Leonardo

LEONARDO DA VINCI (1452–1519) was a man of unique gifts, whose fertile imagination produced images of unequaled vitality and beauty. His drawings and notebooks (pp. 38–39) reveal that "the divine art of painting" was just one of a mass of activities that absorbed him. He was also skilled in anatomy, botany, sculpture, architecture, music, optics, and much else besides. His genius, as Vasari relates, was such that he confounded "the boldest minds." Yet Leonardo "envisaged such subtle, marvelous, and difficult problems that his hands, while extremely skillful, were incapable of ever realizing them." That is why so many of his paintings and projects were never completed, and why his fellow citizens and artistic rivals were prepared to line up in procession to see a wondrous "cartoon" (full-size preparatory drawing), similar to the one opposite, by his hand.

YOUTHFUL GRACE
This detail of *David* by Leonardo's master, Verrocchio, suggests the renowned physical beauty of the young Leonardo.

FLORENTINE MASTER
Born in Vinci, near Florence, Leonardo trained in the busy workshop of Andrea del Verrocchio (p. 26). Leonardo finished his apprenticeship in 1472, when he was entered as an independent master in the register of the Guild of St. Luke (above).

VERROCCHIO'S EXAMPLE
Verrocchio, a Florentine goldsmith, sculptor, and painter, was also one of the most gifted draftsmen of his day, as his eloquent drawing of a girl with elaborately dressed hair demonstrates. He taught his pupils to make exquisite studies from nature, to draw forms in perspective, and to study the nude in various postures. Leonardo was fascinated by the intricate hairstyles that were then so fashionable; his works include similar portraits of girls with plaited tresses, and the intertwining forms of "many designs of knots."

FACE OF AN ANGEL
Leonardo's varied light effects can be seen in this detail. He made a scientific study of light and shadow in nature and also experimented with the light-reflective properties of translucent layers of oil paint. The luster of each hair is delicately picked out, but he avoids the strong, shiny reflections often used by Northern artists – on the whites of the eye, for instance. Instead, a soft light plays over the angel's ethereal features.

MONA LISA
Leonardo; c.1503–6; 30¼ x 20¾ in (77 x 53 cm); oil on panel
The beguiling beauty of this famous portrait derives as much from the haunting mountainous landscape as from the enigmatic Florentine woman who inhabits it. The veiled ambiguity of her smile gives the painting its timeless appeal. Seated high on her balcony, she is at once welcoming and remote.

STUDIES OF NATURE
The studies of plants that appear in the foreground of *The Virgin of the Rocks* show Leonardo's botanical interests. Although the flowers are conventionally symbolic, Leonardo's understanding of their growth and structure is revealed in the movement he has imparted to them. They seem to stir with an inner life.

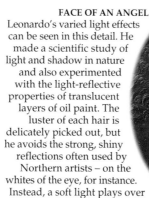

THE VIRGIN OF THE ROCKS
Leonardo; c.1508; 74½ x 47¼ in (189.5 x 120 cm); oil on panel
This, Leonardo's second version of *The Virgin of the Rocks*, was installed in the center of an altarpiece in the Milanese Church of San Francesco in 1508. Certain details were left unfinished, such as the angel's left hand and Christ's back. The image is based on a tale in which the infant Christ and St. John the Baptist meet in the wilderness, where John lives as a child hermit, looked after by an angel. Here Christ (on the right) blesses John. Leonardo has given the scene a mysterious beauty by veiling everything in shadow.

DYNAMIC COMPOSITION

Leonardo uses a complex pyramid of overlapping and intertwining forms to express the interaction between his holy figures. The Virgin is half-seated on the lap of her mother, St. Anne, while Christ's twisting pose unites them. The arc formed by his body links with the Virgin's arm and Anne's shoulder to form a sacred circle. These geometrical rhythms also underlie the way the other forms balance and flow into one another. The figures are compressed into a small space, to powerfully concentrate the overall effect of the cartoon.

LEONARDO'S SIGNS

The emotions of the figures are revealed through their facial expressions and gestures. Christ's right hand is precociously raised in blessing, while with his other hand he cradles his cousin's chin. The face of the Virgin, suffused with light, is gently indulgent and filled with grace. Her mother's expression is smudged in smoky shadow, but her finger, pointing upward, suggests the divine foreknowledge that lies behind her strange smile.

SMOKY TECHNIQUE

The *sfumato* (Italian: "smoky") technique – in which outlines are softened and shadows blurred – was introduced into painting by Leonardo. Although areas of rough outline have been left visible in this preparatory drawing, the *sfumato* effects are clear in the more fully worked upper portion of the composition – particularly in the faces. No doubt the distant mountain landscape and the pebbles in the foreground would have been veiled and softened in the final work; in Leonardo's oil paintings, the outlines all but disappear in a mist of atmospheric color.

The Virgin and Child with St. John the Baptist and St. Anne

LEONARDO *c.1507–8; 55¼ x 42 in (141.5 x 104.6 cm); black and white chalk on tinted paper*
Leonardo's only surviving cartoon may be a variant of a lost drawing that was exhibited in 1501 in Florence: it made such an impression on his contemporaries that some, like the young Michelangelo, tried to mimic Leonardo's astounding compositional skills (in the *Doni Tondo*, p. 55). This later cartoon may be related to an altarpiece on the same theme, made for King Louis XII of France. The design is full size, but it has never been transferred to panel – there are no pinholes in the drawing surface.

PRICKED CARTOON
This detail from Raphael's *Cartoon for an Allegory* shows how holes are pricked along the outlines to transfer a design. The cartoon was placed on a panel and dusted over with powdered charcoal, so that the powder went through the pinholes and stained the surface beneath.

Leonardo's explorations

THE VOLUMINOUS NOTEBOOKS of Leonardo – two of which were discovered as recently as 1965 – provide a fascinating record of his endless inventiveness and the complexity of his genius. They are written in reverse, in his famous "mirror" writing, a style that naturally suited his left-handedness, and are illustrated with explanatory drawings. Alongside his scientific explorations of every facet of perspective, color, light and shade, and human anatomy, there are designs for flying machines, mathematical puzzles, ball-bearing mechanisms, steam cannons (of the type later used in the American Civil War), and even musical instruments. Like other artists of the time, Leonardo adapted his skills as an architect to the profitable area of military engineering, canal building, and weapon design. His letter of introduction to Lodovico Sforza, the Duke of Milan, explains how he can contrive collapsible bridges, machines for draining trenches, siege equipment, armored cars, and multi-barreled guns (ancestors of the modern machine gun). At the end of the letter, he briefly details his peacetime abilities as an architect, sculptor, and painter! His writings lay down a challenge to future generations, "to pursue and invent things anew."

LEONARDO AND MUSIC
An outstanding performer on the *lira da braccio* (above), Leonardo made his own instrument, as well as new types of drums and a keyboard.

DRAWING OF A DELUGE
Leonardo's series of *Deluge Drawings* (c.1515) – which show cataclysmic visions of rain, waves, foam, and whirlpools – are linked to his scientific researches into the dynamics of water, and how its flow has "changed the face and the center of the world." Leonardo was mesmerized by the primeval power of water, which has the potential to wreak universal havoc: "The waters destroy the mountains, fill the valleys, and would reduce the world to perfect sphericalness if they could."

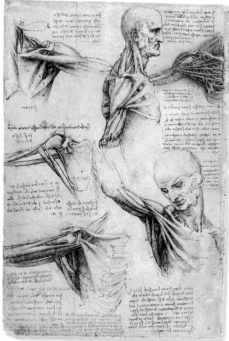

HUMAN ANATOMY
Leonardo planned a treatise on anatomy and carried out dissections of over 30 bodies. Here, he has made a detailed anatomical study of the muscles of the arm. Leonardo regarded the body as the ultimate machine, using its components to solve intricate mechanical problems such as the wiring of a keyboard (based on the tendons of the hand) or the design of a musical recorder (based on the upper larynx).

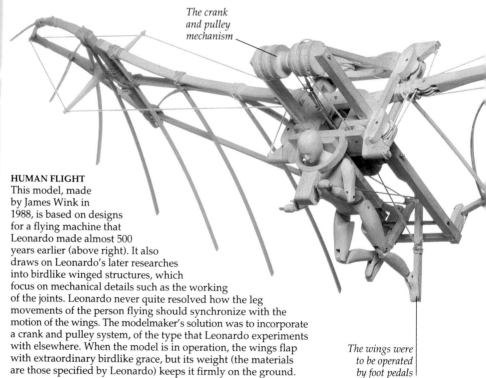

The crank and pulley mechanism

HUMAN FLIGHT
This model, made by James Wink in 1988, is based on designs for a flying machine that Leonardo made almost 500 years earlier (above right). It also draws on Leonardo's later researches into birdlike winged structures, which focus on mechanical details such as the working of the joints. Leonardo never quite resolved how the leg movements of the person flying should synchronize with the motion of the wings. The modelmaker's solution was to incorporate a crank and pulley system, of the type that Leonardo experiments with elsewhere. When the model is in operation, the wings flap with extraordinary birdlike grace, but its weight (the materials are those specified by Leonardo) keeps it firmly on the ground.

The wings were to be operated by foot pedals

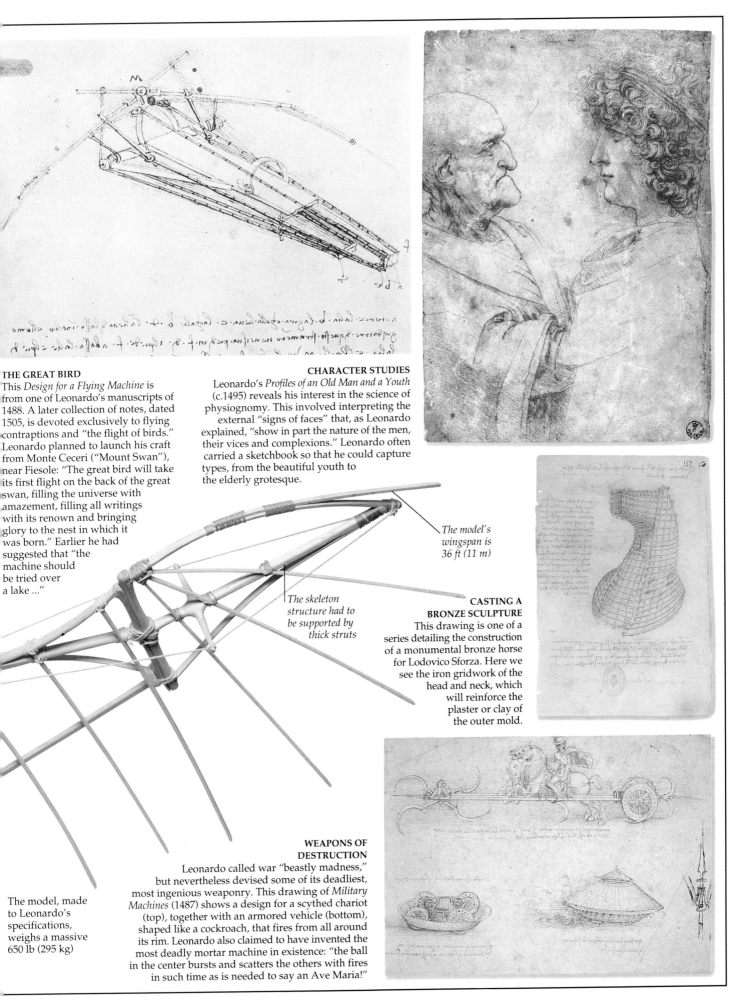

THE GREAT BIRD
This *Design for a Flying Machine* is from one of Leonardo's manuscripts of 1488. A later collection of notes, dated 1505, is devoted exclusively to flying contraptions and "the flight of birds." Leonardo planned to launch his craft from Monte Ceceri ("Mount Swan"), near Fiesole: "The great bird will take its first flight on the back of the great swan, filling the universe with amazement, filling all writings with its renown and bringing glory to the nest in which it was born." Earlier he had suggested that "the machine should be tried over a lake ..."

CHARACTER STUDIES
Leonardo's *Profiles of an Old Man and a Youth* (c.1495) reveals his interest in the science of physiognomy. This involved interpreting the external "signs of faces" that, as Leonardo explained, "show in part the nature of the men, their vices and complexions." Leonardo often carried a sketchbook so that he could capture types, from the beautiful youth to the elderly grotesque.

The model's wingspan is 36 ft (11 m)

The skeleton structure had to be supported by thick struts

CASTING A BRONZE SCULPTURE
This drawing is one of a series detailing the construction of a monumental bronze horse for Lodovico Sforza. Here we see the iron gridwork of the head and neck, which will reinforce the plaster or clay of the outer mold.

The model, made to Leonardo's specifications, weighs a massive 650 lb (295 kg)

WEAPONS OF DESTRUCTION
Leonardo called war "beastly madness," but nevertheless devised some of its deadliest, most ingenious weaponry. This drawing of *Military Machines* (1487) shows a design for a scythed chariot (top), together with an armored vehicle (bottom), shaped like a cockroach, that fires from all around its rim. Leonardo also claimed to have invented the most deadly mortar machine in existence: "the ball in the center bursts and scatters the others with fires in such time as is needed to say an Ave Maria!"

Dürer's pioneering role

THE GERMAN PAINTER and printmaker Albrecht Dürer (1471–1521) was determined to elevate the status of art in the North and gain international recognition as an "artist-painter" rather than a craftsman. He approached these twin tasks with almost missionary zeal: traveling to Italy to seek instruction from Italian Renaissance masters; studying languages and cultivating princes to enhance his social standing; making engravings and woodcuts of unprecedented size and complexity (which were copied by artists all over Europe); and writing important treatises on perspective and human proportions. The son of a goldsmith, Dürer's intellectual and artistic ambitions were fueled by his godfather, the printer and publisher Anthony Koberg, and his friendship with the famous classical scholar Willibald Pirckheimer, who had prompted his study of Italian Renaissance ideas. But it was, above all, Dürer's technical inventiveness and consciousness of his own originality that gave him such a pivotal role in the history of European art.

THE PAINTER'S FATHER
Ascribed to Albrecht Dürer; 1497;
20 x 16 in (51 x 40.3 cm); oil on panel
Only the face of this portrait of Dürer's father is held to be by Dürer. The features are given sharpness and clarity by the emphasis on line and detail.

THE FOUR APOSTLES
Albrecht Dürer; 1526; each panel: 84½ x 30 in
(214.6 x 76.2 cm); oil on panel
Dürer's mature style was dominated by Italian ideals of monumentality and grandeur. These two panels, his last paintings, also reveal his involvement with the new religious ideas of the Reformation (pp. 42–43). Each apostle represents one of the four human temperaments (for example, Paul, shown full face, is melancholic), which suggest different and individual ways of experiencing God.

THE GREAT PIECE OF TURF
Albrecht Dürer; 1503; 16 x 12½ in (41 x 31.5 cm); watercolor and gouache
Dürer studied every detail of nature, approaching even a piece of turf with an analytical eye. This watercolor was executed at the same time as animal studies, which were recorded with similar microscopic exactitude. Such delicacy of observation was translated into an increasingly refined engraving technique (right), in which many details can only be truly appreciated by looking through a magnifying glass.

VIEW OF THE ARCO VALLEY
Albrecht Dürer; 1495; 8¼ x 8¾ in (22.5 x 22.5 cm); watercolor
This watercolor landscape of Arco, on Lake Garda, was executed on Dürer's return from Italy in 1495. Here, the strict accuracy of the individual parts of a view – Dürer's enduring interest – has been sacrificed for the harmonious unity of the overall scheme.

Master printmaker

Dürer's prints show a supreme mastery of their respective mediums. Dürer pushed the technique of line engraving – which had originated in the 15th century in the goldsmith's workshop – to its limits. The line engraving (right) is created by gouging lines in a copper plate with a sharp tool known as a "burin." Ink is then sunk into the grooves and the plate pressed onto damp paper. For the ancient technique of the woodcut (below right), the wooden block was cut away around the sinuous lines of the design, leaving the image raised and ready to be inked (below).

KNIGHT, DEATH, AND THE DEVIL
Albrecht Dürer; 1513; 10 x 7½ in (25 x 19 cm); engraving
This master engraving shows how meticulously and expressively Dürer handled the burin. He used tightly spaced strokes, dots, and networks of dense parallel lines to create velvety shades and tones, as well as atmosphere. The subject is the active power of Christian faith – embodied in the steadfast knight armed with spiritual weapons, who clings to the rocky path of virtue even when threatened by the specter of Death or the Devil.

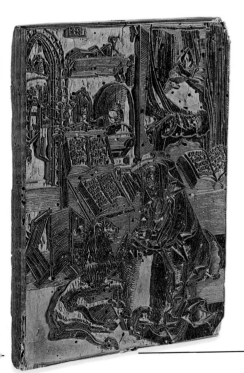

ST. JEROME IN HIS STUDY
Following his apprenticeship in the studio of Michael Wolgemut, Nuremberg's leading painter and book illustrator, Dürer found work designing woodcuts. This frontispiece was made for a collection of St. Jerome's writings, which was published in Basel in 1492 – unlike the later *Knight, Death, and the Devil*, which was designed as a work of art in its own right. The block from which it was printed (left) was cut rather crudely by a professional woodcutter (it is now riddled with wormholes). Within a few years, Dürer was performing the majority of the cutting himself; later, he trained members of his busy workshop in his own dynamic style of woodcutting.

The Reformation

THE RADICAL RELIGIOUS BELIEFS of the German Martin Luther (1483–1546) – which brought about the division of Western Christendom – altered the nature of sacred art. As part of the Holy Roman Empire, Germany was subject to the Catholic Church in Rome, and received papal reprimands for "the foulest abominations and filthiest excesses" of some of its people. Luther resented this emphasis on sin and punishment, and, in 1521, he came into direct conflict with the Papacy over the sale of "indulgences" – documents bought for cash that could be offered in place of doing penance. He believed that salvation could only be granted by the grace of God, not through human works. As Luther's ideas spread, some painters abandoned images of hell and damnation, and art began to reflect the spirit of the new Protestant faith.

THE TEMPTATION OF ST. ANTHONY
Matthias Grünewald; 1515; 98½ x 36½ in (250.2 x 92.7 cm); oil on panel
This scene by the German artist Matthias Grünewald (c.1460–1528) appears on an inner wing of his *Isenheim Altarpiece*, which was painted for an Anthonite hospital order. The story of their patron, St. Anthony, vividly illustrates the medieval belief that the soul could only achieve grace by actively resisting the Devil. Here, his suffering is paralleled by that of the diseased figure on the left.

THE TEMPTATION OF ST. ANTHONY
Hieronymus Bosch; c.1505–10; 52 x 47 in (132 x 119.3 cm); oil on panel
The Northern artist Hieronymus Bosch (c.1450–1516), an orthodox Catholic, had eminent Catholic patrons. He lived in an age beset by anxieties: plague was rife, as were religious and social turmoil, and people believed in physical manifestations of evil, such as witches. An astrological prediction of 1499 had stated that the world would end in 1524: this central panel of Bosch's triptych reveals his pessimism. The kneeling saint in the center is surrounded by temptresses and demons, who personify evil planetary influences and human folly.

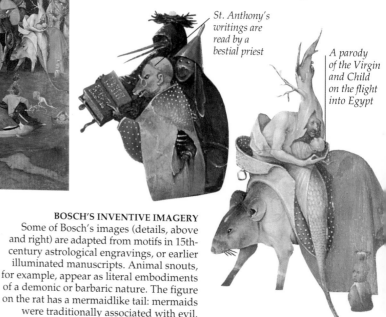

St. Anthony's writings are read by a bestial priest

A parody of the Virgin and Child on the flight into Egypt

BOSCH'S INVENTIVE IMAGERY
Some of Bosch's images (details, above and right) are adapted from motifs in 15th-century astrological engravings, or earlier illuminated manuscripts. Animal snouts, for example, appear as literal embodiments of a demonic or barbaric nature. The figure on the rat has a mermaidlike tail: mermaids were traditionally associated with evil.

ST. ANTHONY IN FRONT OF THE CITY
Dürer was profoundly influenced by Lutheran thought. In this engraving of 1519, he shows the hermit St. Anthony, believed to be the founder of the first monastic order, dressed in a monk's cloak and cowl, drawing moral strength from his inner struggles. This differs from the traditional depiction of him in the desert beset by weird creatures, as in Grünewald's panel (left). Although Grünewald had Lutheran sympathies, he also had Catholic patrons who saw Anthony as an instrument for the Devil to play on. In contrast, Dürer stresses the saint's personal relationship with God and the scholarly nature of his search for spiritual truth.

THE AMBASSADORS
Hans Holbein the Younger; 1533; 81½ x 82½ in (207 x 209.5 cm); oil on panel
This life-size double portrait by the German artist Hans Holbein (1497/98–1543) reflects the change in the intellectual climate brought about by the Reformation: the idea that humanity is no longer prey to its own folly, but has the power to achieve a virtuous state through the pursuit of knowledge. It shows Jean de Dinteville, the French ambassador, and Georges de Selves, Bishop of Lavour, in front of an array of instruments, used for learned pursuits. The strange object at their feet is a human skull shown in distorted perspective. When viewed from a certain angle, it takes a normal shape, serving as a memento mori ("reminder of death") and a warning against pride in knowledge for its own sake.

THE DANCE OF DEATH
A revival of the medieval theme of the Dance of Death also raised questions about the Catholic Church's authority. A skeletal figure of Death visits living individuals from every rung of the social ladder, showing that all humans are equal before death. The most famous example is the series of 40 woodcuts designed by Holbein and printed in 1538 (*The Astronomer* is shown left).

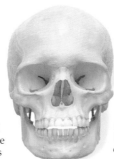

Death's face – a human skull

LUTHER'S BIBLE
Luther's insistence on returning to the original text of the Bible reduced the importance of the numerous tales that had sprung up around the lives of the saints and the Virgin. While outlawed and in hiding (under the protection of Frederick the Wise, the Elector of Saxony), he began his own German translation of the Bible, returning to the original Greek and Hebrew texts. The first Lutheran Bible was printed in 1534, and was hugely influential. Laypeople now had access to its writings, along with the clergy. It received a new edition (left) in 1546 – the year of Luther's death.

The predella shows Luther preaching in front of a crucifix

REFORMATION ALTARPIECE, ST. MARIEN CHURCH, WITTENBURG
Lucas Cranach the Elder; 1547–52; center panel: 47½ x 32 in (120.7 x 81.3 cm), wings: 47½ x 18¼ in (120.7 x 46.4 cm); oil on panel
As court artist to Frederick the Wise, the German artist Lucas Cranach (1472–1553) was the "official" painter of the Protestant cause, although he continued to paint for Catholic patrons. He partly financed the first printing of Luther's Bible, and this altarpiece (completed by Cranach's son, Lucas the Younger) commemorates Luther's teachings.

The Venetian State

Renaissance Venice was one of the richest, most politically enlightened, and secure states in Europe. Her commercial prosperity rested as much on her mainland territories, which included Padua and Bergamo, as on her great sea empire – encompassing lands from Istria nearby, to Cyprus (acquired in 1489). Traditionally a sea-trading capital, where the exotic East mingled with the West, Venice became increasingly embroiled in the political wars in Italy (1494–1530), fought for control of the different states. She emerged proud and "inviolate," her strength due in large measure to the unique stability of her Republican constitution. In the absence of a court, artists benefited from State patronage. No one believed in the supremacy of Venice more than the Venetians themselves; they embellished their buildings and palaces, not just for personal prestige, but to enhance the greatness of the State.

VALUABLE CURRENCY
Artists were lured to Venice by the prospect of being paid in Venetian ducats, one of the strongest currencies on the international market.

THE ROLE OF THE SCUOLE
The Venetian *Scuole* – lay religious associations that administered charitable funds – were important patrons of art: the Scuola Grande di San Marco, which was managed by leading civil servants, employed three of Venice's leading artists for ceremonial duties and to decorate its headquarters (below).

After destruction by fire, the Scuola was rebuilt in 1485 with subsidies from the State

The lower part of the facade was redesigned by Pietro Lombardo

The Doge's Palace

THE DOGE LEONARDO LOREDAN
Giovanni Bellini; c.1501; 24¼ x 17¾ in (61.6 x 45.1 cm); oil and tempera on panel
Bellini has portrayed Leonardo Loredan, Doge from 1501 to 1521. The Doge was the elected ruler of the Republic. Like a modern monarch, he was head of state in name only, ruled for life (he was elected at a "mature" age), and had no political affiliations, other than those of his family. The Doge's Palace (above left) was decorated by the greatest painters of the day: Titian, Tintoretto (pp. 46–47), and Veronese (right).

Sansovino's great reputation temporarily plummeted in 1545, when one of the library's bays collapsed

The columns, arches, sculpted reliefs, and statues revive the splendor of Venice's ancient Roman past

The library is only two stories high, so that it does not compete with the Doge's Palace facing it

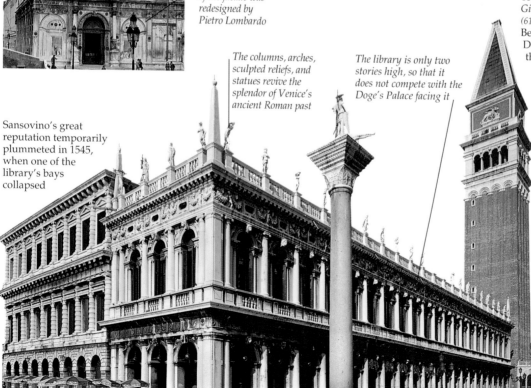

THE MARCIANA LIBRARY
Since Venice was built on a lagoon, its buildings had to be supported by oak piles driven into the mud. Despite the limitations imposed by such an environment, famous architects were drawn to the capital. The Florentine Jacopo Sansovino (c.1486–1570) fled to Venice from the Sack of Rome in 1527 (p. 50) and was made architect to the Republic in 1529. His great library (1537–88) – which the architect Palladio described as "probably the richest building ever built from the days of the ancients up to now" – stands opposite the Doge's Palace on the Piazza San Marco.

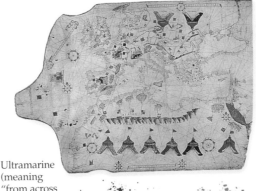

Ultramarine (meaning "from across the seas") was shipped from Afghanistan,

Ultramarine (violet-blue)

Realgar (orange)

Orpiment (yellow)

EXOTIC LUXURIES
Venetian trade in luxury goods from the East included exotic spices, such as nutmeg, mace, and, most importantly, pepper; dyes and pigments – the finest ultramarine and the orange and gold colors used in manuscripts (above); silks; jewelry; medicinal drugs; and ceramics.

Mace

Nutmeg fruit

Ground nutmeg

Ground mace

Long pepper

Peppercorns

ENTHRONED MADONNA WITH SAINTS
Giovanni Bellini; 1505; 16 ft 5 in x 7 ft 9 in (5.00 x 2.36 m); oil on canvas
This altarpiece is still in the Church of San Zaccaria, Venice. It shows the Virgin and Child, absorbed in quiet meditation, surrounded by four imposing saints who occupy the same lofty, atmospheric space. This type of image, known as a *sacra conversazione* (Italian: "a holy communing," between the Virgin, Child, and saints), was given its most intimate, innovative form in Bellini's Venetian altarpieces. The music-playing angel enhances the mood of spiritual harmony.

DECORATIVE RICHNESS
The Venetian taste for sumptuous fabrics, like this silk brocade (below), is reflected in the material splendor of Venetian painting, from the rich draperies, brocades, and decorative oriental rugs to the delight in stylized pattern and decoration (below left).

THE MARRIAGE AT CANA
Paolo Veronese; 1563; 21 ft 10 in x 32 ft 6 in (6.65 x 9.91 m); oil on canvas
Huge canvas pictures became a specialty in Venice, tolerating the damp conditions: this one was painted by Paolo Veronese (1528–88) for the Sacristy of San Giorgio Maggiore. The composition is so crowded with incidental detail – musicians, servants, jesters, dogs, guests in brocaded costumes – that it is difficult to notice Christ sitting quietly in the center. This delight in festivity and everyday pleasures (dining, drinking, music, and conversation) is one of the most characteristic features of Venetian painting.

Titian, master of color

DOLCE'S DIALOGUE
The theorist Ludovico Dolce hailed Titian as the greatest of living painters in his famous *Dialogue on Painting* (1557).

TITIAN (C.1485–1576) WAS THE dominant painter of the Venetian Renaissance, and an artist of unparalleled international stature. He trained under Giovanni Bellini (p. 34) and later joined the workshop of Giorgione (p. 35): several of Titian's early paintings were once believed to be by Giorgione's hand. The novelty of Titian's approach, with its dynamic poses and bravura coloring, asserted itself in one of his first public commissions – the great *Frari Altarpiece*. This established his reputation as a startlingly original colorist who employed color rather than line as the main ingredient of his painting. It also revealed his ability to give an intensely physical form to spiritual rapture. His sensual style found its most exuberant outlet in his mythological paintings, including *Bacchus and Ariadne*, created for the Duke of Ferrara's castle, and the later erotic *poesie* ("painted poems"), made for King Philip II of Spain. Titian's patrons were wide-ranging: he was not only court painter to the Holy Roman Emperor, but was commissioned by the government and Church in Venice, the Gonzaga family from Mantua, and the Roman Farnese family of Pope Paul III. Titian's reputation ensured his position as Venice's rival to Florence's Michelangelo.

THE ASSUMPTION AND CORONATION OF THE VIRGIN
Titian; 1516–18; 22 ft 8 in x 11 ft 10 in (6.91 x 3.61 m); oil on panel
The colossal *Frari Altarpiece* was made for the high altar of the great Venetian Church of Santa Maria Gloriosa dei Frari. Titian's vision of the Assumption and Coronation, when the Virgin was raised up to heaven after her death and crowned, was so unconventional that the friars who commissioned the work were unsure whether to accept it. What no doubt disconcerted them were the emotionally charged poses, the boldness of the composition, and the rich sensuality of color. The Virgin is virtually silhouetted by a blazing halo of light, witnessed by the apostles, whose confusion and amazement is dramatized by deep shadows.

The complex, double-twisting pose of the Virgin is the first of its type in Venetian art

COLOR TRIANGLE
Much of the impact of the *Frari Altarpiece* is created through the color structure. The composition is divided into two large sections – a heavenly circle above, and the rectangular block of the apostles below (in a shape that suggests the Virgin's sarcophagus). Titian uses a pattern of color to unite the two areas: a tall triangle, formed by the vermilion robes of the two apostles at the base, the Virgin's gown, and God's cloak, sweeps the eye up to the top of the altarpiece. He also used the finest pigments, juxtaposing them in contrasting patches of color, which are carefully balanced to suggest that we are viewing the event in natural lighting conditions.

ARIADNE'S CONSTELLATION
The sparkling circle of stars in the sky (top left in the painting) symbolizes the moment when Bacchus tossed Ariadne's jeweled crown to the heavens.

FIGURES IN MOTION
The forward momentum, which culminates in the balletic leap of Bacchus in the center, is set in motion by the crowd of figures behind him. The satyr, who brandishes a calf's leg, leans into the picture and is overlapped by the powerful, striding figure of a follower entwined in snakes.

NARRATIVE DETAIL
The departing ship of Theseus is shown on the sea in the distance.

BACCHUS AND ARIADNE
Titian; 1520–23; 69 x 75 in (175.2 x 190.5 cm); oil on canvas
This is one of three mythological paintings completed by Titian for Alfonso d'Este's *Camerino d'Alabastro* (Italian: "Alabaster Chamber") in his castle at Ferrara, in Italy. Raphael (p. 48) was originally commissioned to paint the story of Bacchus and Ariadne, but on his death the commission passed to Titian. The painting is based on tales told by the Roman poets Ovid and Catullus, and shows the wine god Bacchus coming to the aid of Ariadne, the daughter of King Minos. She had been abandoned by her lover, Theseus, on the island of Naxos. Elements of the story are represented throughout the painting (left; above right), while the composition focuses on the figure of Bacchus. The unbridled energy of his pose (he is positioned in midair) is set off by the brilliance of the coloring and the expansive landscape. Bacchus is followed by his carousing retinue – some of their poses are borrowed from classical statues; the figure with snakes is based on the *Laocoön* (p. 50).

ORIGINS OF THE MILKY WAY
Tintoretto; c.1578; 58¼ x 65 in (148 x 165.1 cm); oil on canvas
Titian's paintings created a vogue for mythological subjects in Venice in the 16th century. Tintoretto (1518–94) was greatly indebted to him, but he was also critical of the older master's methods, writing his own formula for success on the wall of his room: "The drawing of Michelangelo and the coloring of Titian." This mythological picture, like the religious works that Tintoretto painted, shows off his energetic draftsmanship and his love of dramatic light effects.

PORTRAIT OF A MAN
Titian; c.1511; 32 x 26 in (81.2 x 66.3 cm); oil on canvas
Titian excelled as a portraitist, immortalizing the features of many of the most powerful men in Europe: he painted magnificent portraits of the Emperor Charles V; Francis I, the King of France; and Philip II of Spain. This early work may be a self-portrait, and it is a supremely confident demonstration of Titian's artistic powers. One of the most impressive features is the luxurious blue silk sleeve, which is bathed in light and seems to drape over the illusionistic stone parapet, out of the picture space. Another is the calm, self-assured gaze of the sitter, which unwaveringly meets our own.

The High Renaissance

THE YEAR 1500 MARKS a subtle shift in artistic style and objectives. The new phase, which is popularly known as the High Renaissance, is usually associated with the careers of the Italian giants Michelangelo, Raphael, and Titian. To Vasari, writing in 1550, the key to the new artistic style was *"grazia,"* meaning a refined grace and ease of manner. Even the most contrived details were made to appear effortless and unforced. In technical terms, oil was the ideal medium for displaying this *grazia* – colors could be blended to create effects of softness and charm. It was perfect, too, for expressing the "boldness" of each artist's personal style, which had become so highly valued. Individuality was also measured by the artist's inventiveness and the scope of his imaginative powers: no challenge was too great, no pose too complex, no scale too grand!

PORTRAIT OF BALDASSARE CASTIGLIONE
Raphael; c.1514–15; 32¼ x 26 in (82 x 66 cm); oil on canvas
The great Raphael (1483–1520) painted this portrait of his friend Castiglione, who wrote the *Book of the Courtier* (1528; below). Like many High Renaissance portraits, it is painstakingly designed to look both simple and sophisticated. The count displays the inner calm required of a gentleman.

THE ART OF THE COURTIER
Castiglione's influential treatise, which describes an ideal of courtly behavior at the Italian ducal court of Urbino (below), expresses the idea that art should conceal the work that goes into its creation. The artist, like the courtier, was to appear effortlessly accomplished in all fields.

The Ducal Palace of Urbino

Urbino enjoyed fame as a cultural center under the Montefeltro dukes

THE APOLLO BELVEDERE
The elegant pose of this Roman statue provided artists with a model of ease, grace, and power in movement. Dating from the 2nd century A.D., the statue is a marble copy of an ancient Greek bronze. It was found in the late 15th century and became the pride of Pope Julius II's new Belvedere Collection of sculpture (p. 58).

The delicately joined hands are based on life studies

THE ARCHANGEL RAPHAEL WITH TOBIAS
Pietro Perugino; c.1500–5; 44½ x 22¼ in (113.3 x 56.5 cm); oil and tempera on panel
The Umbrian Perugino (c.1450–1523) was one of the most successful Italian painters in the 1480s and 1490s. The charm and sweetness of his figures were imitated by his young assistant, Raphael, who was to combine these qualities with Leonardo's new, grand Florentine style (pp. 36–37). Perugino was praised for his graceful method of coloring in oils, which he had mastered by studying Flemish examples (pp. 20–21). In this panel, which is part of an altarpiece, Perugino's skill in the painting of light effects can be seen in the luminous reflections of the flesh, the fish's scales, and the boy's lustrous hair (detail, left). Tobias is artfully posed in the classical manner – with his body curving to take the weight on one leg – but a preparatory drawing shows that both figures were drawn from life: a boy and an assistant had posed.

HE GARVAGH MADONNA

aphael; c.1508–10; 15¼ x 13 in (38.7 x 32.7 cm); oil on panel
aphael's paintings of the Virgin and Child present an
mage of idealized nature. Following the practice of the
me, Raphael has selected the most beautiful elements
om nature (drawing from life) and combined them
vith the best details and ideas from works by other
nasters: for example, the pyramidical figure composition
borrowed from Leonardo. The gesture of the Virgin
olding her drapery comes
om Roman sculpture
senators were shown
olding their togas
a similar way.

THE BATTLE OF ISSUS

Albrecht Altdorfer;
1529; 62½ x 47½ in
(158.4 x 120.3 cm); oil on panel
With growing confidence,
artists extended their range
of subject matter, even
attempting to capture the
dazzling atmospheric
effects of nature and
portraying its infinite
grandeur. While Italian
painters represented
landscapes, clouds, night
skies, and the shimmering
sun as part of the human
environment, the German
artist Albrecht Altdorfer
(c.1480–1538) presented
humanity as a tiny "speck"
in the vast eternal scheme
of things, its struggles and
strivings dwarfed by the
cosmic forces of nature.
This spectacular battle
scene, with its fantastic,
seething sky (detail, below
right), is more astonishing
for being represented on a
relatively small scale. In
his bird's-eye view of
the scene, Altdorfer has
transcended the limitations
of his panel to convey the
world's true magnitude.

The glory of the setting
sun evokes the splendor
of nature —

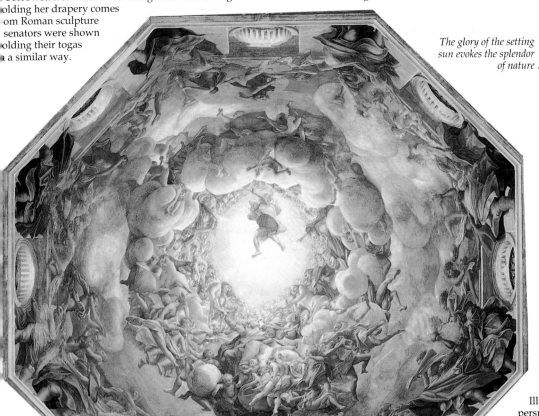

The windows flood
the interior of the
dome with light,
adding to its
visionary impact

ASSUMPTION OF THE VIRGIN

Correggio; 1526–30; 35 ft 10 in x
39 ft 2 in (10.93 x 11.95 m); fresco
While Altdorfer's modestly sized
panel provided no obstacle to his
grand vision, many artists realized
that largeness of scale could only
add to the impact of their works. The
High Renaissance saw the creation
of numerous works on a daringly
colossal scale, from Michelangelo's
David (p. 54) to the architecture
of the new St. Peter's (p. 51) and
Correggio's great illusionistic dome
paintings in Parma Cathedral (left).
Illusionism – where the painter uses
perspective tricks to give the illusion of
an alternative reality – presented one of the
most obvious opportunities for artists to display
their skill. The northern Italian painter Correggio
(c.1494–1534), who learned many of his tricks from
Mantegna, surpassed him in boldness and ingenuity,
solving every problem with stylish ease. The effect is
miraculous: the eye spirals upward from the apostles
on the dome's lower rim, through angels and cloud-
borne cherubim, to the Virgin in the heavens.

Rome's renewal

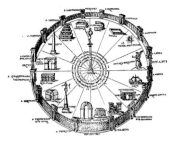

WHEN RAPHAEL ARRIVED in Rome in 1508, Pope Julius II had already embarked on his ambitious plans to restore the ailing city to its ancient grandeur. Rome had only become the continual residence of the papacy under Pope Nicholas V (1447–55), when alterations were begun. Now cardinals and wealthy individuals, encouraged by major tax concessions on property, busily erected splendid palaces, churches, and buildings – while Roman remains were unearthed during construction work. The Sienese banker Agostino Chigi, a financier to the popes, built the Villa Farnesina; even its stables, designed by the young Raphael, were calculated to be grander than a palace. The major architectural project of the period was the building of the new St. Peter's, which consumed the talents of its first architect, Donato Bramante (c.1444–1514), and others, including Michelangelo and Raphael. It devoured marble from Rome's ancient ruins, although Leo X (Julius II's successor) had put Raphael in charge of preserving Rome's archaeological heritage. The flurry of artistic activity was abruptly interrupted by the Sack of Rome in 1527, when French troops ravaged the city, forcing its artists and citizens to flee.

LAOCOON
2nd–1st century B.C.; height: 8 ft (2.45 m); marble
The exciting discovery in a vineyard on the Esquiline Hill, on January 14, 1506, of the antique sculpture known as the *Laocoön* had a huge impact on artists in Rome. Michelangelo and the architect Giuliano da Sangallo saw it when it was still in the ground, and recognized it as the ancient Greek group described by Pliny as "a work to be preferred to all that the arts of painting and sculpture have produced."

The group shows the Trojan priest Laocoön and his sons being crushed to death by snakes

THE TRIUMPH OF GALATEA
Raphael; 1511; 116 x 88½ in (295 x 225 cm); fresco
The airy garden rooms of Chigi's Villa Farnesina (below) were used for lavish entertaining. They were decorated with mythological scenes in the manner of ancient imperial Rome: Raphael's famous fresco of *Galatea* complements scenes in the same *loggia* (an external gallery) by other artists, including the Sienese architect and painter Baldassare Peruzzi (1481–1536). Peruzzi painted Chigi's horoscope on the ceiling vault, as well as designing the villa itself. The source for Raphael's fresco was "Verses for the Joust of Giuliano de' Medici" by Politian (p. 33), in which he describes an engraved image of the sea nymph Galatea – riding on a shell pulled by dolphins and accompanied by sea creatures and *amorini* (little "Cupids") – which appears on the doors of the Palace of Venus. It seems that Raphael was emulating the beauty of a lost masterpiece.

THE VILLA FARNESINA
The Villa Farnesina (1508–11) was designed by Peruzzi in the classical style of a Roman country house with two projecting wings. He also painted the false perspective views of the *Salone delle Prospettive* inside. Peruzzi's elegant style led to his appointment as a co-architect of St. Peter's (above right) on Raphael's death in 1520.

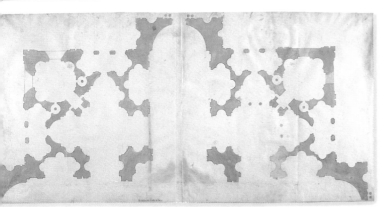

BRAMANTE'S PLANS
Bramante's plan of 1506 (left) and Caradosso's bronze medal (right), which was struck to commemorate the design for the exterior, give us some idea of the scale of the architect's ambitions for the new St. Peter's. The church was planned in the shape of a Greek cross (having four equal "arms"), with a tall turret at each outer corner. It was to be crowned by a massive dome on the huge scale of Rome's ancient Pantheon.

This shows Bramante's original design: note the differences in the finished version (below)

The completed dome was much higher than the shallow dome planned

The new St. Peter's

The old Basilica of St. Peter's stood over the alleged grave of St. Peter, a shrine for all Christendom. It was erected in A.D. 324 by Constantine the Great and survived in dilapidated form until Julius II's reign, when it was pulled down to make way for a church of unsurpassed splendor. The foundation stone for the new St. Peter's was laid in 1506, and its design entrusted to the esteemed, but elderly, architect Bramante. It was to occupy ten architects before its final completion, over 120 years later.

MICHELANGELO'S CONTRIBUTION
Bramante constructed the piers (large supporting pillars) and arches to the dome, but the building did not begin to take its present form (right) until 1546, when Michelangelo was made architect by Pope Paul III. He worked on it until his death in 1564, designing the back of the church and the dome (completed by Giacomo della Porta in 1593).

The dome's jutting rims and plain niches on the drum make it look like a piece of solid sculpture

Bramante adopted the circular form of ancient temples instead of the square crucifix form of Renaissance churches

A RENAISSANCE TEMPLE
Bramante's *Tempietto* (Italian: "Little Temple") at San Pietro in Montorio, Rome (1502), is considered to be the embodiment of High Renaissance architecture. It marks the spot where St. Peter was believed to have been crucified, and looks more like a sculptural monument than a building. Perfectly round and unadorned by ornament, it has the austere, monumental dignity of a full-size classical temple: artists of the High Renaissance tried to re-create both the style and spirit of ancient Rome.

DECORATIVE SCHEMES
The fresco decoration of Cardinal Bibbiena's Vatican *loggia*, completed in 1516 by Raphael and his chief assistant, Giovanni da Udine, was inspired by decorative paintings found in the subterranean rooms of the Golden House of Nero and in a Roman ruin near the Church of San Pietro in Vincoli. Their light, graceful ornamental forms – a mixture of plants, human figures, and fantastic creatures – were called "grotesques," from *grotte* (Italian: "caves").

Raphael's Vatican rooms

RAPHAEL'S FAST-GROWING reputation in Florence brought him to the attention of Pope Julius II in Rome. By 1509 he was hard at work on a suite of papal apartments – his three *stanze* (rooms) – in Rome's magnificent Vatican palace, while Michelangelo labored under lock and key on the Vatican's Sistine Chapel ceiling nearby (pp. 56–57). The first room Raphael completed, the so-called *Stanza della Segnatura* (Room of the Signature) established his reputation immediately. Its frescoes, with their graceful classical poses and grand compositions, have been copied by countless artists over the centuries. Raphael created a vigorous dramatic style in the second room, the *Stanza d'Eliodoro* (Room of Heliodorus). The aged Pope died before its completion, and the final *Stanza dell'Incendio* (Room of the Fire) was painted, with the help of pupils, under Pope Leo X.

PHILOSOPHY
Raphael depicted the theme of the *Stanza della Segnatura* i four medallions on the ceilin – female figures represent Philosophy (above), Theolog Poetry, and Jurisprudence. Under each is the fresco tha brings its learned discipline to life; the ancient thinkers (below) appear under *Philosophy* (above).

The School of Athens

RAPHAEL *c.1510–12; lunette: 25 ft 4 in (7.72 m) at base; fresco*
The *Stanza della Segnatura* was probably intended to be Pope Julius II's private library. Appropriately, the ceiling shows the four disciplines (above right) under which books would have been classified, while the wall frescoes depict all the literary heroes of classical and Christian times: the ancient philosophers of *The School of Athens* (right) appear on the wall opposite learned theologians, discussing the mystery of the Sacrament; and the great poets of *Parnassus* (far right) face the lawmakers.
The famous *School of Athens* was painted in about 1510–12, at a time when the first section of Michelangelo's ceiling was unveiled (August 14, 1511) – the bulky figure resting on a block in the foreground, which is not in the preparatory cartoon, seems to imitate Michelangelo's prophets and sibyls (pp. 56–57).

LOGICAL POSITIONS
The careful placing of numerous figures within a deep perspective setting looks back to the methods of Ghiberti (p. 14). Raphael has extended similar precision to the poses of each individual figure. Every gesture and movement (based on classical sculpture) is as logically determined as the mathematical perspective construction.

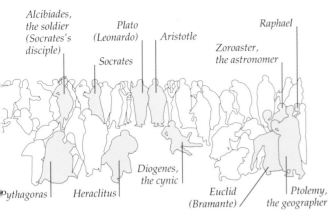

Alcibiades,
the soldier
(Socrates's
disciple)

Plato
(Leonardo)

Aristotle

Raphael

Socrates

Zoroaster,
the astronomer

Diogenes,
the cynic

Pythagoras   Heraclitus

Euclid
(Bramante)

Ptolemy,
the geographer

ANCIENT PHILOSOPHERS
Various figures have been identified in *The School of Athens*. In the
center are the Greek philosophers Plato (modeled on Leonardo) and
Aristotle. Their gestures – Plato points to the heavens, while Aristotle
extends his hand toward earthbound reality – indicate the sources
of their ideas. Raphael has even included himself among the pupils.

POPE JULIUS II
*Raphael; c.1511–12; 42½ x 31¼ in
(108 x 80.7 cm); oil on panel*
During his reign, Pope Julius
II (1503–1513) set Rome at the
very center of Italy's cultural
achievements. He not only
commissioned Michelangelo's
Sistine ceiling and Raphael's
stanze, but also founded the
famous Belvedere Collection
of sculpture (p. 58) and began
the new St. Peter's (p. 51). In
the political sphere, he was a
brilliant financial reformer,
an astute diplomat, and a
skillful military campaigner.
Raphael's fine portrait shows
the Pope in the year before
his death. His chair back is
topped with acorns, from
the oak emblem of the della
Rovere family, to which he
belonged. (These acorns also
appear on the Sistine ceiling.)

THE LIBERATION OF ST. PETER FROM PRISON
Raphael; c.1512–13; lunette: 21 ft 8 in (6.60 m) at base; fresco
The *Stanza d'Eliodoro* – named after one of its frescoes, the *Expulsion of Heliodorus* –
shows miraculous events in the history of the Christian Church. The most remarkable
scene is the *Liberation of St. Peter*, which is painted around a window, making the fresco
appear even darker. As St. Peter sleeps in his cell, an angel appears in a blaze of light,
causing the chains to fall from his hands. The saint is led out (on the right), while the
soldiers (on the left) stumble, dazzled by the radiance. The episode was particularly
relevant, for Pope Julius II's troops had recently liberated Italy from the French, and
he had given thanks in the Church of San Pietro in Vincoli ("St. Peter in Chains").

COPYING RAPHAEL
During Raphael's
lifetime, the fame of
his compositions was
spread by the engraver
Marcantonio Raimondi
of Bologna (c.1480–1534),
who offered his services
to Raphael in Rome.
This engraving shows
the *Parnassus* fresco
of Apollo, muses, and
poets in the *Stanza della
Segnatura*, and was
made after a finished
drawing that differs in
details from the fresco.

53

Michelangelo's "divine" powers

THE FLORENTINE SCULPTOR, painter, poet, and architect Michelangelo Buonarroti (1475–1564) pushed the artistic ideals of his generation to their physical and stylistic extremes. Born into minor nobility, he learned fresco techniques in the workshop of Ghirlandaio (p. 13) and trained as a sculptor. In his youth, he copied frescoes by Giotto and Masaccio and studied Donatello's sculpture. Inspired by their heroic example, and that of antique sculpture, he developed an ideal based on the physical expressiveness of the male nude. The grace and awe-inspiring scale of his works had a huge impact: Michelangelo unwittingly fostered the cult of the genius with superhuman powers, transforming the way artists regarded themselves and their works.

MICHELANGELO
This bust of Michelangelo appears on his tomb in Santa Croce, Florence, which was designed by Giorgio Vasari. It is to Vasari that we owe the idea of Michelangelo as the artist "who surpasses them all."

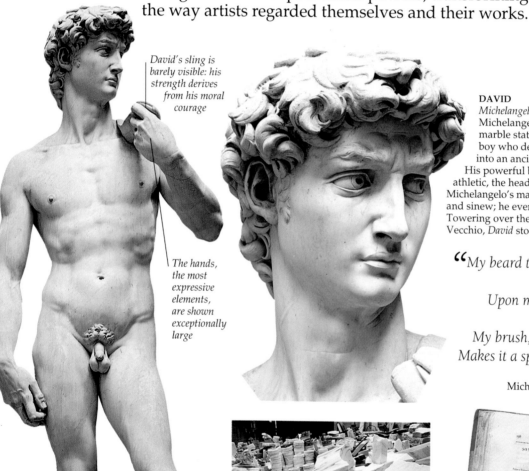

David's sling is barely visible: his strength derives from his moral courage

The hands, the most expressive elements, are shown exceptionally large

DAVID
Michelangelo; 1501–4; height: 13 ft 5 in (4.09 m); marble
Michelangelo's *David* is the largest free-standing marble statue since classical times. The shepherd boy who defeated the giant Goliath is transformed into an ancient hero of unrivaled grace and beauty. His powerful body is both indolently sensual and athletic, the head (detail, left) is noble and idealized. Michelangelo's mastery of anatomy is seen in every muscle and sinew; he even details the bulging veins in the hands. Towering over the people at the entrance to the Palazzo Vecchio, *David* stood as a symbol of Florence's supremacy.

"*My beard toward Heaven, I feel the back of my brain,
Upon my nape I grow the breast of a Harpy;
My brush, above my face continually,
Makes it a splendid floor by dripping down.*"

Michelangelo, Sonnet 64, verse 2

THE CARRARA MARBLE QUARRIES
The dimensions of *David* were dictated by a massive shallow block of marble, quarried in 1466, in which a figure of a giant had been blocked out, botched, and then abandoned. Michelangelo rose to the challenge. For the *Julius Tomb* (opposite), however, he spent eight months at the Italian marble quarries of Carrara, selecting suitable blocks.

MICHELANGELO'S POETRY
Michelangelo was one of the greatest poets of his age. His sonnets poignantly, and sometimes humorously, express his spiritual and artistic struggles. The sonnet above, written in 1511, light-heartedly relates the very real physical torments of painting the Sistine Chapel ceiling (pp. 56–57).

THE DONI TONDO
Michelangelo; c.1506–8; diameter: 47¼ in (120 cm); tempera on panel
The *Doni Tondo*, the only completed panel painting by Michelangelo to survive, was commissioned by Angelo Doni to mark his marriage to Maddalena Strozzi. The complex, interlocking poses of the Holy Family were based on a cartoon by Leonardo and were designed to echo the curves of the *tondo* (Italian: "round painting"). The artfully posed male nudes in the background may have been included to show Michelangelo's skill in this field.

THE LAURENTIAN LIBRARY STAIRCASE
Michelangelo's design for the architectural framework of the *Julius Tomb* led to a lifelong fascination with architecture. For the Medici, he built the New Sacristy of San Lorenzo in Florence and began work on the Laurentian Library next door. Its staircase (above) was later executed to one of Michelangelo's designs, and shows how he has begun to use forms expressively, freeing them from their structural purpose. Michelangelo's most important commission was the completion of the new St. Peter's, which was largely realized in his lifetime.

THE TRAGEDY OF THE JULIUS TOMB
In 1505, Pope Julius II summoned Michelangelo to Rome to create a magnificent free-standing tomb for him on the scale of the famous mausoleums of antiquity. Fired with enthusiasm for the scheme, destined to take a prominent place in the old St. Peter's, Michelangelo hastened to Carrara to select the marble for 40 figures, which were to be more than life-size. The Pope's interest in the project soon evaporated (probably due to the plan to build a new St. Peter's). Julius II died in 1513, and the ill-fated project staggered to completion in 1545. It had dwindled to the shrunken tomb (above) that now stands in San Pietro in Vincoli in Rome. Only *Moses* (c.1515; right) and the niches (1506) are by Michelangelo's hand.

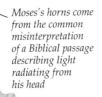

Moses has the *terribilità* (Italian: "awesome power") so admired by Michelangelo's contemporaries

Moses's horns come from the common misinterpretation of a Biblical passage describing light radiating from his head

THE CROSSED-LEG CAPTIVE
Michelangelo; 1527–28; height: 9 ft 1 in (2.77 m); marble
This unfinished slave, intended for the *Julius Tomb*, reveals Michelangelo's method of sculpting by cutting into the front of the block, rather than from all sides. To the artist it seemed that he was freeing the emerging figure – the embodiment of his idea – from its prison of stone.

The Sistine ceiling

MICHELANGELO'S SISTINE CHAPEL ceiling in the Vatican represents the summit of his achievement. It was commissioned by Pope Julius II in 1508, partly to make amends for abandoning the project of the *Julius Tomb* (p. 55). Many of the titanic figures intended for the tomb seem to have been included on the ceiling vault. The Pope originally wanted Michelangelo to depict the twelve apostles and cover the old, blue, star-spangled ceiling with a fashionable, ornamental scheme. But Michelangelo declared that this would be "a poor thing," and a more spectacular, erudite plan was devised. Majestic Old Testament prophets and ancient sibyls (female seers) now flanked the main vault, which was painted with the epic story of Noah and the Creation.

THE BELVEDERE TORSO
The twisted poses of the *ignudi* – idealized nudes at the corners of the main scenes – were based on this torso (c.50 A.D.).

THE DELPHIC SIBYL
Michelangelo; 1509; 137¼ x 149½ in (350 x 380 cm); fresco
The classical sibyls, who uttered prophecies and oracles, were named after their places of origin: the young Delphic Sibyl is associated with the Greek oracle at Delphi. Surviving drawings show that Michelangelo's sibyls were based on muscular male models. This image, from the blackened ceiling before it was cleaned, shows the "stony" coloring that deceived viewers into thinking the figures were painted to resemble marble sculpture.

COLOR INSPIRATION
Michelangelo is seen as the creator of the "artificial" Mannerist (pp. 60–61) style of coloring. He inspired the early Mannerist master Pontormo (p. 61) to use vivid hues of unearthly delicacy.

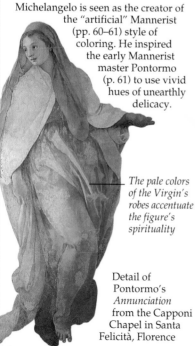

The pale colors of the Virgin's robes accentuate the figure's spirituality

Detail of Pontormo's *Annunciation* from the Capponi Chapel in Santa Felicità, Florence

Plan of the Sistine ceiling

North Wall: Life of Christ

South Wall: Life of Moses

David and Goliath	Zechariah	Judith and Holofernes
The Prophet Joel	Drunkenness of Noah	Delphic Sibyl
Zorobabel	The Flood	Josias
Erythraean Sibyl	Sacrifice of Noah	The Prophet Isaiah
Ozias	Fall and Expulsion	Ezekias
The Prophet Ezekiel	Creation of Eve	Cumaean Sibyl
Roboam	Creation of Adam	Asa
Persian Sibyl	Separation of Waters from the Earth	The Prophet Daniel
Salmon	Creation of Sun, Moon, and Plants	Jesse
The Prophet Jeremiah	Separation of Light from Darkness	Libyan Sibyl
Punishment of Haman	Jonah	The Brazen Serpent

Section shown right

West Wall; Altar; Michelangelo's *Last Judgment* (1535–41)

Color Key:

- Central panels: the story of Noah and the Creation
- Prophets and sibyls
- *Ignudi*
- Corner spandrels: Old Testament scenes
- Vaulting compartments: ancestors of Christ
- Simulated bronze medallions

THE MEANING OF THE CEILING
The overall theme of the ceiling has been much discussed. It is now thought that the episodes from the Old Testament and the sayings of the prophets and sibyls are linked because, according to a medieval tradition, they foretell the coming of Christ. For this reason, Christ's ancestors are shown. The scheme was designed to complement earlier wall paintings of the lives of Moses and Christ by other artists.

MICHELANGELO'S TRUE COLORS
This shows the *Delphic Sibyl* after cleaning, and vividly displays the loveliness and originality of Michelangelo's coloring. The draperies are painted in radiant contrasting hues, which imitate the color shifts of shot silk. Such *cangiante* (Italian: "changing") coloring had previously been reserved largely for the robes and wings of angels. Michelangelo, however, uses it for the entire ceiling, endowing his figures with grace and vitality. He had intended to enrich the coloristic effect by retouching areas in ultramarine blue and gold, but the Pope's impatience to see the ceiling completed meant such details had to be sacrificed.

🖌 **HUMAN DIVERSITY**
Prophets and sibyls, seated on weighty architectural thrones, face each other across the ceiling. The cornices of the thrones, held up by *putti* (Cupid-like infants), support the marble seats above, on which the 20 famous *ignudi* are posed. These figures represent an astonishing range of ages, body types, and facial expressions, and display the "extremes and perfection" of Michelangelo's abilities.

🖌 **THE CREATION**
In the famous *Creation of Adam*, the might of God is physically embodied in his muscular body and his stern, fatherly gaze. The immense power that flows from his finger conjures up the words of the hymn sung on papal election day: "Thou ... Finger of the paternal right hand ... Let thy light inflame our senses, Pour thy love into our hearts ..."

🖌 **STARTLING VIEWPOINTS**
The Separation of Light from Darkness shows God in dramatic foreshortening (p. 63); we see the underside of his bearded chin and his upturned nose. Such a viewpoint could have been considered unseemly, but God is shown in this way so that he can be seen from the altar directly below. As the priest conducting Mass directed the eyes of his congregation toward Heaven, they would feel they shared in the first divine revelation.

The Sistine Ceiling (section)

MICHELANGELO *1508–12; 42 ft 8 in x 118 ft (13 x 36 m); fresco*

Michelangelo made over two hundred preliminary drawings for the ceiling, which were painstakingly made into cartoons. These full-size working designs were laid against the wet plaster, which was applied to the ceiling each day, and the outlines were traced with a stylus (grooves can still be seen). Michelangelo frescoed the huge vault alone, having dismissed his helpers because their work was so inferior. He painted from a standing position in great discomfort, and refused to admit anyone into the chapel as he labored. Work was often interrupted; early sections became moldy – pigments reacted with the plaster – and he ran out of funds. In 1512, after four and a half years of intolerable exertion, the ceiling was finally unveiled. The artist's vision of God's power and humanity's spiritual awakening left everyone speechless with admiration.

The North and Italy

FOLLOWING DÜRER'S EXAMPLE (pp. 40–41), Northern artists of the early 16th century began to study and absorb the ideas of the Italian Renaissance. In Augsburg, the wealthy commercial center of Germany, painters like Hans Holbein the Younger (p. 43) sought inspiration from northern Italy. Antwerp, with its busy port and resident foreign merchants, evolved an eclectic style that was to dominate 16th-century Northern art, in which Flemish and Italian elements were fused. The "Romanists," Jan Gossaert (c.1478–1532) and Jan van Scorel (1495–1562), looked directly to the antique and to its Italian intermediaries like Leonardo, Raphael, and Michelangelo. Gossaert was the first Northern artist to study Roman antiques through the support of a patron, while van Scorel succeeded Raphael as the curator of the Belvedere Collection of antiquities in the Vatican.

ROME'S BELVEDERE COLLECTION
The Romanists regarded the ancient past as an idyllic era. Gossaert's interests coincided with those of his patron, Philip of Burgundy, who took the artist with him on his diplomatic mission to the Vatican in about 1508. There, Gossaert made a record of the classical sculpture in the Belvedere Collection. This collection had been formed in 1503 by Pope Julius II, who had begun to place the newly excavated classical works of art in the Belvedere Court (shown in this engraving). By the time van Scorel was put in charge of the collection in 1522, it included treasures like this Roman sculpture of *Venus Felix and Amor* (right), placed there in 1509.

Like Italian artists, Gossaert and van Scorel were influenced by the idealized forms of antique sculpture

NEPTUNE AND AMPHITRITE
Jan Gossaert; 1516; 74 x 48¾ in (188 x 123.8 cm); oil on panel
In 1515, Gossaert began a series of mythological paintings for Philip of Burgundy's castle, working with the Venetian printmaker and painter Jacopo de' Barbari (c.1440–1516). Barbari died just as work began, and Gossaert took over, creating in his *Neptune and Amphitrite* the first nudes of Flemish painting to be genuinely classically inspired. The poses are taken from Barbari's well-known print of *Mars and Venus* (below), but Gossaert has made the forms heavier and more sensuous. The monumentality of the figures is enhanced by the illusionistic ancient architecture that they so solidly inhabit.

MARS AND VENUS
Jacopo de' Barbari was a significant figure in the blending of Northern and Italian styles. He made his name in northern Europe, working at the courts of Emperor Maximilian and Frederick the Wise of Saxony in Germany, and for Margaret of Austria and Philip of Burgundy in the Netherlands. His mythological prints helped to spread the concept of the Italian nude in the North and profoundly influenced Dürer, who used them in his own studies of the human nude (p. 30).

A GROTESQUE OLD WOMAN
After Quinten Massys; 1510/20; 25¼ x 18 in (64.1 x 45.4 cm); oil on panel
Antwerp's leading painter, Quinten Massys (c.1465–1530), was a veritable magpie in his borrowings from different artistic styles. This portrait (made famous in the 19th century, when it was used to illustrate the Duchess in Lewis Carroll's *Alice's Adventures in Wonderland*) was inspired by Leonardo's caricatures.

BONIFACIUS AMERBACH
Hans Holbein the Younger; 1519; 11¼ x 11 in (28.5 x 27.5 cm); tempera on panel
This portrait by Holbein seems naturalistic but is actually carefully contrived. Painted on his return from northern Italy, it has certain Venetian characteristics, such as the atmospheric contrasts of light and shade. However, Venetian portraits of this period were themselves indebted to Northern examples.

THE PRESENTATION OF CHRIST IN THE TEMPLE
Jan van Scorel; c.1530–35; 45 x 33½ in (114 x 85 cm); oil on panel
Van Scorel's refined blending of Italian and Northern elements has earned him the nickname of the "Northern Raphael." He experienced Italian art firsthand, visiting Venice in about 1519, and taking up residence in Rome from 1522 for his prestigious Vatican appointment under Pope Adrian IV, a fellow Dutchman. This picture shows how thoroughly he had studied the art and architecture of Rome. The temple is in the style of Bramante (p. 51), and the proportions and draperies of the figures reveal an awareness of Italian style. However, the naturalistic relationship between the figures and the airy space they occupy, as well as the emphasis on the architecture itself, is more Northern than Italian.

AN ELDERLY COUPLE
Jan Gossaert; c.1520–25; 18 x 26½ in (45.7 x 67.3 cm); oil on vellum
This double portrait of an elderly man and his wife draws on a long tradition of Flemish portraiture, where penetrating observation of an individual (often close to caricature) is combined with monumentality. Half-length double portraits, in which the sitters' differences are subtly emphasized, were popular in Italy, Germany, and the Netherlands from the mid-15th century. Here, the raised and lowered gazes suggest active and passive personalities.

Mannerism

THE LABEL "MANNERISM" – from the Italian *maniera*, meaning "style" – is often applied to art in the period from about 1520 to 1580. Mannerist works are refined, sophisticated, and technically accomplished: they are deliberately stylish, making a cult of the beautiful and delighting in bizarre, fanciful imagery. However, there is a problem with the Mannerist label, in that it has come to symbolize an abrupt break with the ideals of the High Renaissance. Mannerist art has been seen as decadent and neurotic, at odds with the ideals of harmony and grace established by preceding generations. Now, modern definitions of Mannerism regard it as more of a continuation and elaboration of trends set in motion by the High Renaissance. It draws on, for example, the suave grace and theatricality of Raphael's mature compositions, as well as Michelangelo's skill in portraying the male nude, from the taut muscular forms and artful poses to his stylized borrowings from the antique (a constant source of inspiration).

SELF-PORTRAIT IN A CONVEX MIRROR
Parmigianino; 1524;
diameter: 9½ in (24.3 cm); oil on panel
This self-portrait, by the Italian Parmigianino (1503–40), is a self-consciously clever image. It is both natural and contrived, faithfully reproducing the mirror's strange distortions.

THE BATTLE OF CASCINA
Aristotile da Sangallo; 1542; 30 x 52 in (76.2 x 132 cm); grisaille on panel
Michelangelo was the artist most admired by the Mannerists – this is a copy of his famous lost cartoon of *The Battle of Cascina*. Michelangelo's cartoon, made in competition with Leonardo's *Battle of Anghiari* for the decoration of the Grand Council Chamber in Florence, shows the bathing soldiers startled by the call to battle, an ideal subject to show off his mastery of the nude. It is a storehouse of idealized and tortuously complex poses – all of which demonstrate astonishing accomplishment.

TWISTING MOVEMENT
This detail shows the ostentatious and deliberate difficulty of the poses that Michelangelo set himself.

CUPID COMPLAINING TO VENUS
Lucas Cranach the Elder; 1530; 32 x 21½ in (81.3 x 54.6 cm); oil on panel
In the North, Cranach developed a refined style that has parallels with Italian Mannerism. Like his Italian colleagues, Cranach was influenced by prevailing aristocratic tastes: in 1505, he succeeded Jacopo de' Barbari as court painter to Frederick the Wise, and worked in an atmosphere of relaxed elegance and sophisticated pleasures. *Cupid Complaining to Venus* exudes a mannered grace and sensuality: the eyes even have a feline quality. His Venus, however, is portrayed as a fashionable beauty, complete with hat and jewelry, rather than an idealized Italianate nude.

An Allegory with Venus and Cupid

AGNOLO BRONZINO *1540–45; 57½ x 45¼ in*
(146.1 x 116.2 cm); oil on panel

This sophisticated image by the great Mannerist Agnolo Bronzino (1503–72) symbolizes erotic passion. Stylistically, it is indebted to Michelangelo and his *Doni Tondo* (p. 55), but Bronzino has exchanged the physical and emotional intensity of the Holy Family for a languid sensuality and cool detachment. Venus and her incestuous lover Cupid are shown with idealized and elongated bodies, unaware of the destructive nature of their love. The half-girl/half-beast offering a honeycomb shows how love's sweetness also has a sting in its tail.

BIZARRE CREATIONS
This shows a fantastic mask of Venus by Giovanni Battista Rosso (1495–1540), designed for one of King Francis I's elaborate pageants at Fontainebleau, in France. It exhibits the Mannerist taste for bizarre ornament.

UNSEEING FACES
The masks, with their vacant eyes, symbolize deceit (detail, above), and also emphasize the atmosphere of artificiality.

JOSEPH IN EGYPT
The difference between the early Renaissance ideals of Ghiberti (p. 14) and those of an early Mannerist like Jacopo Pontormo (1494–1556) can be seen in their versions of the same story. Ghiberti uses perspective space to provide a logical storytelling framework, while Pontormo takes a more daring approach.

JOSEPH IN EGYPT
Jacopo Pontormo; c.1519;
38 x 43 in (96.5 x 109.5 cm); oil on panel
Pontormo's picture reveals how radically artistic objectives have changed over the Renaissance period. Ghiberti's narrative is clear, his composition harmonious, and the space is carefully arranged. In Pontormo's scene, the staircase flamboyantly sweeps nowhere, the figures are grouped here and there, and the different episodes of the story are difficult to isolate. The emphasis is on pattern and fantastic invention, in keeping with the decorative nature of the work.

Chronology

1266/67 Birth of Giotto.

1302 Papal Bull proclaiming papal supremacy over national rulers.

1302–10 Giovanni Pisano working on Pisa Cathedral pulpit.

1304 Birth of Petrarch.

1308 Dante begins his *Divine Comedy*.

1309 Papacy moves from Rome to Avignon because of unrest.

c.1305 Giotto paints Arena Chapel.

1311 Duccio's *Maestà* carried in procession to Siena Cathedral.

1317 Venetian fleet makes longest sea voyage to date.

1319 Death of Duccio.

1321 Death of Dante.

1337 Death of Giotto.
Beginning of Hundred Years War between France and England.

1338 Ambrogio Lorenzetti paints *Good Government* frescoes, Palazzo Pubblico, Siena.

c.1339 Birth of Rogier van der Weyden.

1340 Simone Martini working at papal court in Avignon.

1344 Death of Simone Martini.

1348 The Great Plague devastates Europe; probably claims life of Ambrogio Lorenzetti.

1353 Publication of Boccaccio's *Decameron*.

1364 Charles V becomes King of France.

c.1370 Birth of Gentile da Fabriano.

1374 Death of Petrarch.

1375 Death of Boccaccio.

1376 Return of papacy to Rome.

1377 Birth of Brunelleschi.
Richard II becomes King of England.

1378 Birth of Ghiberti.
Rival line of popes elected; Western Church divided.

c.1386 Birth of Donatello.

1397 Birth of Uccello.

1400 Birth of Luca della Robbia.
High point of International Gothic style.

1401 Birth of Masaccio.

1405/6 Death of Claus Sluter.

c.1406 Birth of Fra Filippo Lippi.

c.1415/20 Birth of Piero della Francesca.

1416 Limbourg Brothers decorate *Les Très Riches Heures du Duc de Berry*.

1419 Philip the Good becomes Duke of Burgundy.

1420 Brunelleschi begins work on the dome of Florence Cathedral.

1424 Masaccio and Masolino begin the Brancacci Chapel frescoes.

1427 Death of Gentile da Fabriano.

c.1428 Death of Masaccio.

1431 Birth of Mantegna.

1434 Medici family become dominant faction in Florence.
Van Eyck paints *The Arnolfini Marriage*.

1435 Birth of Verrocchio.
Birth of Giovanni Bellini.
Alberti completes *On Painting*.

1441 Death of van Eyck.

1444 Birth of Bramante.

1445 Donatello begins *Gattamelata*.
Birth of Botticelli.

1446 Death of Brunelleschi.

1447 Death of Masolino.
Nicholas V becomes Pope.

1449 Birth of Ghirlandaio.

c.1450 Rogier van der Weyden's probable trip to Italy.
Gutenberg's invention of printing using movable type.

1452 Birth of Leonardo da Vinci.
Ghiberti completes Baptistery doors.

1453 Hundred Years War ends.
Turks capture Constantinople; the end of the Byzantine Empire.

1455 Death of Ghiberti.
Death of Fra Angelico.
Wars of the Roses begins in England.

1457 Death of Andrea del Castagno.

1460 Birth of Grünewald.
Birth of Antonio del Pollaiuolo.

1464 Death of Van der Weyden.

c.1465 Birth of Quinten Massys.

1466 Death of Donatello.

1467 Charles the Bold becomes Duke of Burgundy.

1469 Birth of politician Machiavelli.
Lorenzo de' Medici rules Florence.
Death of Fra Filippo Lippi.

1471 Birth of Dürer.
Election of Pope Sixtus IV.

1472 Birth of Cranach the Elder.

1475 Birth of Michelangelo.
Death of Uccello.
Death of Dieric Bouts.

1476/78 Birth of Giorgione.

c.1478 Birth of Gossaert.
Giuliano de' Medici murdered during Pazzi conspiracy.

c.1480 Birth of Altdorfer.
Piero della Francesca writing mathematical treatises (1480s).

c.1481 Pacher completes *St. Wolfgang Altarpiece*.

1482 Death of Hugo van der Goes.
Death of Luca della Robbia.
Sixtus IV summons artists to Rome (including Botticelli, Perugino, and Ghirlandaio) to decorate Sistine Chapel.

1483 Van der Goes's *Portinari Altarpiece* arrives in Florence.
Birth of Martin Luther.
Birth of Raphael.
Charles VIII becomes King of France.
Richard III becomes King of England.

1485 Birth of Titian.
Alberti's *De Re Architectura* published.

Henry VII becomes King of England.

1486 Maximilian I elected King of Germany.

1488 Death of Verrocchio.

1489 Venice acquires Cyprus.

1492 Death of Piero della Francesca.
Innocent VIII elected Pope.
Columbus discovers West Indies.

1494 Political Wars in Italy.
Medici exiled from Florence.
Death of Ghirlandaio.
Birth of Pontormo.
Dürer makes first trip to Italy.

1495 Death of Cosimo Tura.
Birth of Jan van Scorel.

1497/98 Birth of Hans Holbein the Younger.

1498 Death of Antonio del Pollaiuolo.

c.1500–5 Bosch paints *St. Anthony Triptych*.

1501 Leonardo's famous cartoon (now lost) exhibited in Florence.
Michelangelo begins *David*.

1502 Leonardo appointed as Cesare Borgia's chief architect and military engineer.
Bramante completes *Tempietto*.

1503 Election of Pope Julius II.
Birth of Bronzino.
Birth of Parmigianino.

1505 Dürer makes second journey to Italy (returns 1507).
Giorgione paints "landscape," *Tempesta*.

1506 Discovery of the *Laocoön*.
Death of Mantegna.
Foundation stone laid for new St. Peter's.

1508 Michelangelo begins work on the Vatican Sistine ceiling.

1509 Raphael begins work on the Vatican *stanze*.
Henry VIII becomes King of England.

1510 Death of Giorgione.

1511 Birth of Vasari.

1512 Sistine ceiling unveiled.
Fall of Florentine Republic.

1513 Death of Pope Julius II.
Leo X elected Pope.
Medici restored in Florence.

1514 Death of Bramante.

1515 Grünewald completes *Isenheim Altarpiece*.
Doge's Palace completed in Venice.

Francis I becomes King of France

1516 Death of Bosch.
Death of Giovanni Bellini.

1517 Beginning of Reformation in Germany.

1518 Birth of Tintoretto.

1519 Death of Leonardo.
Charles V (King of Spain) becomes Holy Roman Emperor.

1520 Death of Raphael.

1521 Diet of Worms: Luther condemned by Church.
Death of Dürer.

1523 Death of Perugino.

1524 Death of Joachim Patenier.

1527 Sack of Rome by French imperial forces.
Death of Machiavelli.

1528 Publication of Castiglione's *Book of the Courtier*.
Birth of Veronese.
Death of Grünewald.
Publication of Dürer's treatise *On Human Proportion*.

1529 Sansovino made architect to the Venetian Republic.

1530 Correggio completes dome paintings in Parma Cathedral.
Death of Quinten Massys.

1532 Death of Gossaert.

1533 Holbein paints *The Ambassadors*.

1534 Luther's Bible published.
Henry VIII becomes head of Church of England, breaking with Rome.

1538 Publication of Holbein's *Dance of Death*.
Death of Altdorfer.

1540 Death of Parmigianino.

1543 Death of Holbein.

1545 Counter-Reformation begins.

1546 Death of Martin Luther.

1550 Publication of first edition of Vasari's *Lives of the Most Excellent Painters, Sculptors, and Architects*.

1553 Death of Cranach.

1556 Death of Pontormo.

1558 Elizabeth I becomes Queen of England.

1562 Death of van Scorel.

1564 Death of Michelangelo.

1572 Death of Bronzino.

1576 Death of Titian.

1588 Death of Veronese.

1594 Death of Tintoretto.

View of Florence in the 15th century

Glossary

Altarpiece A religious work standing on or at the back of an altar table.

Annunciation The Angel Gabriel's announcement to the Virgin that she "shall conceive and bear a Son" and give him the name Jesus (Luke: 1: 26–38). This represents the moment of Christ's Incarnation (his embodiment in flesh).

Assumption The Virgin's bodily ascent to heaven, following her burial.

Byzantine Art relating to the Byzantine era, dating from the establishment of the Roman Empire in the East (A.D. 476), in the time of the Christian Emperor Constantine, to the fall of its capital Constantinople (the ancient Greek city of Byzantium) in 1453.

Painting in fresco

Cartoon In fine art, refers to a full-scale preparatory drawing on heavy paper, from the Italian *cartone*, meaning "cardboard."

Classical Art of Greek and Roman times, or stylistic qualities inspired by that art.

Egg tempera A technique in which powdered color in water is bound in a medium of egg (as opposed to oil, for instance). The egg binds the paint particles together and makes the paint adhere to the paint surface. As the proteins in the egg harden, the colors form a tough skin and acquire a velvety sheen.

Foreshortening The method by which the intervals of a perspective "pavement" or the parts of an object are diminished, so that they appear shorter and narrower as they recede.

Fresco From the Italian word for "fresh"; in this method of wall painting, powdered colors in water are usually applied to damp plaster. As the lime in the plaster dries and the water evaporates, a hard crystalline surface forms in which the color is bound.

Gesso A smooth white preparatory surface in panel painting, made up of gypsum and animal glue.

Gothic A style of art and architecture in northern Europe, dating from the 12th to the 16th century. The term was invented by Renaissance Italians to describe the barbarous German style of architecture (Gothic comes from "Goths" – the Germanic tribes who helped destroy the Roman Empire).

Guild An independent association made up of bankers, professionals, artisans, or manufacturers. Guilds were responsible for maintaining standards and recruitment.

Maestà An altarpiece featuring the Virgin "in majesty" – enthroned and surrounded by saints and angels.

Mass The celebration of the central Christian sacrament of the Eucharist (Greek: "Thanksgiving"), in which consecrated bread and wine, believed to be the body and blood of Christ, ritually perpetuate the meaning of Christ's sacrifice.

Oil In this technique, powdered pigment is mixed with a medium of slow-drying oil, such as linseed or walnut, which absorbs oxygen from the air, forming a transparent skin that locks the color in.

Passion The sufferings of Christ in his last week on earth: in art, scenes showing Christ's Flagellation, crowning with thorns, carrying of the cross, Crucifixion, and death.

Predella Long, horizontal plinth of an altarpiece, often decorated with painted panels.

Relief From the Italian word for "raised." Sculpture that projects from a back panel, which is an integral part of it. Alternatively, a quality in painting that mimics the effects of relief sculpture, using light and shade to make an image appear to project three-dimensionally from the background.

Featured works

Look here to find the location of, and complete details about, the works featured in the book.

This section also includes photographic acknowledgments, although further information can be found under "Acknowledgments" (p. 64).

Every effort has been made to trace the copyright holders and we apologize in advance for any unintentional omissions. We would be pleased to insert the appropriate acknowledgment in any subsequent edition of this publication.

Key: *t*: top; *b*: bottom; *c*: center; *l*: left; *r*: right

Abbreviations:
AC: Arena Chapel, Padua; **BAL:** Bridgeman Art Library; **BL:** By Permission of the British Library; **BM:** The Trustees of the British Museum, London; **CC:** Chiesa del Carmine, Florence; **KM**: Kunsthistorisches Museum, Vienna; **MD:** Museo dell'Opera del Duomo, Florence; **ML:** Musée du Louvre, Paris; **NG:** Reproduced by Courtesy of the Trustees of the National Gallery, London; **NGW:** © 1994 National Gallery of Art, Washington; **SC:** Scala; **UF:** Uffizi, Florence; **WI:** Warburg Institute, University of London

Front cover: clockwise from top left: *St. Anthony in Front of the City* (p43); *Tempietto* (p51); *Philosophy* (p52); *The Virgin and Child with St. John the Baptist and St. Anne* (p37); *The Magdalen Reading* (p20); *Self-portrait* (p7); Gonzaga *History of the Punic Wars* (p26); *David* (p54); *The Baptism of Christ* (p31) **Inside front flap:** *b*: *Gattamelata* (p26); *The Agony in the Garden* (pp34–35) **Back cover:** clockwise from top left: *The Arnolfini Marriage* (p20); *The Annunciation* (p23); *Putto and Dolphin* (p27); *Cantoria* (p15); *The Archangel Raphael with Tobias* (p48); Bust of Macchiavelli (p12); *Introduction of the Cult of Cybele at Rome* (pp26–27); Florence Cathedral (p12); Caradosso's medal of the new St. Peter's (p51); *The Deposition* (p24); *Bacchus and Ariadne* (p47);

p1 (Half Title): *The Doni Tondo* (p55) **p2:** *tl*: Caradosso's medal of the new St. Peter's (p51); *tr*: Fragment of *Mappemonde* (p45); *tcl*: Model of Leonardo's flying machine (pp38–39); *cl*: *The Wilton Diptych* (p16); *cr*: *The Deposition* (p24); *bl*: *Laocoön* (p50); *bcl*: Detail from *Gates of Paradise* (head of Ghiberti) (p14); *br*: *Vitruvian Man* (p30) **p3 (Title Page):** *tl*: *St. Jerome in a Rocky Landscape* (p35); *c*: *The Assumption and Coronation of the Virgin* (p46); *tr*: *Joseph in Egypt* (p14; p61); *bl*: *The Expulsion* (p19); *br*: *Moses* (p55) **p4:** *tl*: *Portrait of Baldassare Castiglione* (p48); *cl*: *The Youthful David* (p23); *bl*: *Portinari Altarpiece* (p21); *tr*: Woodcut, *St. Jerome in His Study* (p41) *br*: Reliquary of San Domenico, Bologna (p24) **p5**: *br*: *St. Anthony in Front of the City* (p43)

Pages 6–7 What is the Renaissance?
p6: *c*: *Tazza Farnese*, "The Fertility of Egypt," Greco-Egyptian, Museo Nazionale, Naples/SC; *bl*: *The Birth of Venus*, Botticelli, UF/SC **p7:** *tr*: *Self-portrait*, Dürer, Alte Pinakothek, Munich/SC; *cr*: *Christ as Ruler of the Universe, the Virgin and Child, and Saints*, Byzantine artists, the apse of Monreale Cathedral, SC; *b*: *Pietà*, Michelangelo, St. Peter's, Rome/SC

Pages 8–9 The impact of Giotto
p8: *tl*: *Arena Chapel*, SC; *tr*: *The Annunciation*, aisle window, Cologne Cathedral, Dombauverwaltung, Cologne; *cr*: *The Golden Legend*, Jacobus da Voragine; *br*: *The Meeting at the Golden Gate*, Giotto, AC/SC **p9:** *tl* (detail): *The Meeting at the Golden Gate*, Giotto, AC/SC; *tr* (detail), *bl*: *The Kiss of Judas*, Giotto, AC/SC; *cl*: *Navicella*, Beatrizet, © WI; *cr*: *Inconstancy*, Giotto, AC/SC

Pages 10–11 Painting in Siena
p10: *tr*: Siena Cathedral, SC; *l*: Reconstruction of Duccio's *Maestà* (front), after John White; *cr*: *The Annunciation*, Duccio, NG **p10–11:** *b*: *Allegory of Good Government: Effects of Good Government in the City and Its Countryside*, Ambrogio Lorenzetti, Palazzo Pubblico, Siena/SC **p11:** *tr, tl* (detail): *The Annunciation*, Martini and Lippo Memmi, UF/SC; *cl*: Executing punched decoration, NG; *cr*: Modern ring punching tools

Pages 12–13 Renaissance Florence
p12: *tr*: *View of Florence*, 1887 (copy of 1470 woodcut, *Veduta della Catena*), Francesco and Raffaello Petrini, Museo di Firenze com'era, Florence; *cr*: Bust of Brunelleschi, Andrea di Cazzara Cavallanti, MD; *c*: Pulleys used in the construction of Florence Cathedral, MD; *bl*: Dome, Florence Cathedral, SC; *br*: Right aisle, Santo Spirito, Florence **p13:** *tr, cl* (details), *tl*: Tornabuoni Chapel, Santa Maria Novella, Florence; *cr*: Coats of arms; *bl*: *Dante Standing Before Florence*, Domenico di Michelino, MD/SC, Florence; *br*: Bust of Machiavelli, Palazzo Vecchio, Florence

Pages 14–15 Early Renaissance sculpture
p14: *tr*: *The Moses Fountain*, Sluter, Photo © Jean Luc Duthu, inventaire générale – SPADEM © DACS 1994; *c* (detail), *cl*: Baptistery doors (1425–52), Ghiberti; *cr*: *Joseph in Egypt*, Baptistery doors (1425–52), Ghiberti, MD; *b*: Relief, Nanno di Banco **p15:** *l*: *St. George*, Donatello, Bargello, Florence/SC; *bl*: *St. George and the Dragon*, Donatello, relief below *St. George*; *cr* (detail), *tr*: *Cantoria*, Luca della Robbia, MD/SC; *br*: Sculpting tools

Pages 16–17 The courtly style
p16: *tr* (detail): *The Bear and Boar Hunt*, Devonshire Hunting Tapestry, Courtesy of the board of trustees of the Victoria and Albert Museum, London; *cl*: *The Wilton Diptych*, NG; *bl*: *The Wilton Diptych* (reverse), NG; *br*: *April*, from *Les Très Riches Heures du Duc de Berry*, Pol de Limbourg, Musée Condé, Chantilly/Giraudon **p17:** *tr* (detail), *b* (predella panel), *c*: *Adoration of the Magi*, Gentile da Fabriano, UF/SC

Pages 18–19 The Brancacci Chapel
p18: *tr*: Frontispiece of Pliny's *Natural History*, Biblioteca Medicea Laurenziana, Florence; *b* (detail), *c*: *The Healing of the Cripple and The Raising of Tabitha*, Masolino, CC/SC **pp18–19:** *b*: *The Tribute Money*, Masaccio, CC/SC **p19:** *tl*: *Final Judgement*, Giovanni Pisano, pulpit, Pisa Cathedral, SC; *c*: *Temperance*, Giovanni Pisano, Pisa Cathedral, SC; *r*: *The Expulsion*, Masaccio, CC/SC; *bc*: *The Temptation*, Masolino, CC/SC

Pages 20–21 Flemish naturalism
p20: *bl, cr, br* (details), *l*: *"The Arnolfini Marriage"* – full title, *The Portrait of Giovanni (?) Arnolfini and His Wife Giovanna Cenami (?)*, Jan van Eyck; *tr*: *A Man in a Turban*, Jan van Eyck; *bc* (detail): *The Magdalen Reading*, Rogier van der Weyden, NG **p21:** *tl, tc*, (details), *tr*: *The Magdalen Reading*, Rogier van der Weyden, NG; *bl, br* (details), *c*: *Portinari Altarpiece*, Hugo van der Goes, UF/SC

Pages 22–23 The artist's craft
p22: *tr*: Page of Cennino Cennini's *Il Libro dell'Arte*, Biblioteca Medicea Laurenziana/Photo Donato Pineider; *l*: *St. Luke Painting the Virgin and Child*, Follower of Quinten Massys, NG; *c*: Commission contract for *The Coronation of the Virgin* by Enguerrand Quarton, © Photo Daspet, Villeneuve-les-Avignon; *cr*: *The Art of the Apothecary* from the Latin Manuscript *Apuleius Dioscorides*, Eton College Library/BAL; *bc* (detail): Reverse of *St. Paul*, Bernardo Daddi, NGW, Andrew W. Mellon Collection **p23:** *t*: *The Annunciation*, Fra Filippo Lippi, NG; *cl*: *The Birth of St. John the Baptist*, Giovanni di Paolo, NG; *bl*: *The Nerli Cassone*, Zanobi di Domenico, Jacopo del Sellaio, Biagio d'Antonio, Courtauld Galleries, London (Lee Bequest); *br*: *The Youthful David*, Andrea del Castagno, NGW, Widener Collection

Pages 24–25 Images of devotion
p24: *tr*: Reliquary of San Domenico, Bologna, SC; *c*: *Prediche Vulgare*, woodcut, Fra Roberto Caracciolo, WI; *br* (details), *cr*: *The Deposition*, Fra Angelico, Museo di San Marco, Florence/SC; *bc* (detail), *bl*: *The Virgin and Child with Saints Francis and Sebastian*, Carlo Crivelli, NG **p25:** *tr* (detail), *c*: *The Deposition*, Rogier van der Weyden, Museo del Prado, Madrid; *bl*: *St. Wolfgang Altarpiece*, Michael Pacher, St. Wolfganger Kunstverlag, St. Wolfgang, Austria

Pages 26–27 Classical inspiration
p26: *tr*: *Christ before Pilate*, Jacopo Bellini, ML, Département des Arts Graphiques/RMN; *cl*: *Equestrian Statue of Gattamelata*, Donatello, SC; *c*: *Arch of Titus*, SC; *cr*: Gonzaga *Latin History of the Punic Wars*, Lionardo Bruni, BL **pp26–27:** *b*: *The Introduction of the Cult of Cybele at Rome ("The Triumph of Scipio")*, Andrea Mantegna, NG **p27:** *tl*: *The Death of Orpheus*, Albrecht Dürer, Hamburger Kunsthalle; *tc*: *Putto and Dolphin*, Andrea del Verrocchio, Palazzo Vecchio, Florence/SC; *tr*: *Hercules and Antaeus*, Antonio del Pollaiuolo, Bargello, Florence/SC

Pages 28–29 The "invention" of perspective
p28: *tl*: Medal of Alberti by Matteo de' Pasti, BM; *tr*: *Etienne Chevalier with St. Stephen*, left-hand panel of *The Melun Diptych*, Jean Fouquet, Bildarchiv Preussischer Kulturbesitz/Staatliche Museen zu Berlin, Gemäldegalerie/Photo: Jörg P. Anders; *cl*: *The Draftsman's Net*, woodcut from *Treatise on Measurement*, Albrecht Dürer, 1538 revised edition; *bl, b*: *The Hunt in the Forest*, Paolo Uccello, Ashmolean Museum, Oxford **p29:** *tl, bl*: *The Adoration of the Kings*, Bramantino, NG; *bl*: Computer-generated perspective drawing of *The Adoration of the Kings*, NG

Pages 30–31 Harmony and beauty
p30: *tr*: Lettering from *On the Just Shaping of Letters*, Albrecht Dürer, Dover Publications, Inc., New York; *cr*: Palazzo Rucellai, Florence, Leon Battista Alberti, Visual Arts Library, London; *bl*: *Vitruvian Man*, Leonardo da Vinci, Accademia, Venice/SC; *c*: Page from *On Human Proportion*, Albrecht Dürer; *bc*: Page from *De Prospettiva Pingendi*, Piero della Francesca, Biblioteca Palatina, Parma **p31:** *tl, cr*: *The Baptism of Christ*, Piero della Francesca, NG; *bl*: Title page, *Theorica Musice*, Franchino Gafurio, Naples, 1480, WI; *br*: Diagram of Euclid's Proposition 16, Book 4

Pages 32–33 Botticelli and mythology
p32: *tr*: Page from *Fasti*, Ovid, Biblioteca Riccardiana, Florence; *cl*: Medici coat of arms; **pp32–33:** *bl* (detail), *b*: *Primavera*, Sandro Botticelli, UF/SC **p33:** *tl, cl, c*: details of *Primavera*; *cr*: *Lorenzo de' Medici Receiving Calendimaggio Celebrants*, Anon, woodcut from *Canti Carnascialeschi*; *bc*: Medal of Guarino da Verona, BM; *br*: *An Allegorical Figure*, Cosimo Tura, NG

Pages 34–35 The rise of landscape
p34: *l, cl* (details), *tl*: *The Entombment*, Dieric Bouts, NG **pp34–35:** *b*: *The Agony in the Garden*, Giovanni Bellini, NG **p35:** *tl*: *The Agony in the Garden*, Andrea Mantegna, NG; *tr*: *The Valley of the Arno, near Florence*, Leonardo da Vinci, Department of Prints and Drawings, UF/SC; *cr*: *St. Jerome in a Rocky Landscape*, ascribed to Joachim Patenier, NG; *br*: *Tempesta*, Giorgione, Accademia, Venice/SC

Continued on p. 64

Index

Pages 36–37 The genius of Leonardo
p36: *tl* (detail): *David*, Andrea del Verrocchio, Bargello, Florence/Alinari; *tr* (detail): Register of the Academy of St. Luke, State Archives, Florence/SC; *cl*: *Study of a Lady's Head*, Andrea del Verrocchio, BM; *bl*: *Mona Lisa*, Leonardo da Vinci, ML; *c, bc* (details), *br*: *The Virgin of the Rocks*, Leonardo da Vinci, NG **p37**: *t*: *The Virgin and Child with St. John the Baptist and St. Anne*, Leonardo da Vinci, NG; *br*: Detail from *Cartoon for an Allegory ("Vision of a Knight")*, Raphael, NG

Pages 38–39 Leonardo's explorations
p38: *tr*: *Lira da braccio*, A. Andrea, KM; *c*: *Drawing of a Deluge*, Leonardo da Vinci, The Royal Collection © 1994 Her Majesty Queen Elizabeth II; *bl*: *Anatomical Study of the Muscles of the Arm*, Leonardo da Vinci, The Royal Collection © 1994 Her Majesty Queen Elizabeth II; *br*: Model of Da Vinci's flying machine, designed and constructed by James Wink, Tetra Assoc. 1988/Hayward Gallery, London/Photo: Ian Hessenberg **p39**: *tl*: *Design for a Flying Machine*, Leonardo da Vinci, Bibliothèque de l'Institut de France/Photo: Bulloz; *tr*: *Profiles of an Old Man and a Youth*, Leonardo da Vinci, Department of Prints and Drawings, UF/SC; *cr*: *Casting of a Monumental Horse*, Leonardo da Vinci, Biblioteca Nacional, Madrid; *br*: *Military Machines*, Leonardo da Vinci, BM

Pages 40–41 Dürer's pioneering role
p40: *tl*: *The Painter's Father*, ascribed to Albrecht Dürer, NG; *cr*: *The Four Apostles*, Albrecht Dürer, Alte Pinakothek, Munich/SC; *bl*: *The Great Piece of Turf*, Albrecht Dürer, Graphische Sammlung Albertina, Vienna **p41**: *tl*: *View of the Arco Valley*, Albrecht Dürer, ML/SC; *tr*: *Knight, Death, and the Devil*, Albrecht Dürer; *bl* (woodcut), *br* (print): *St. Jerome in His Study*, Albrecht Dürer, Oeffentliche Kunstsammlung Basel, Kupferstichkabinett/Photo: Martin Bühler

Pages 42–43 The Reformation
p42: *tr*: *The Temptation of St. Anthony*, Matthias Grünewald, © Musée d'Unterlinden, Colmar/Photo: O. Zimmermann; *bc, br* (details), *l*: *The Temptation of St. Anthony*, Hieronymus Bosch, Museo Nacional de Arte Antiga, Lisbon/BAL **p43**: *tl*: *St. Anthony in Front of the City*, Albrecht Dürer, Archiv für Kunst und Geschicte, Berlin; *tr*: *The Ambassadors*, Hans Holbein, NG; *cl*: *The Astronomer* from *The Dance of Death*, Hans Holbein, Mary Evans Picture Library; *bl*: Title page, *New Testament*, Martin Luther, 1546, Archiv für Kunst und Geschichte, Berlin; *br*: *Reformation Altarpiece*, Lucas Cranach the Elder, St. Marien of Wittenburg/Archiv für Kunst und Geschichte, Berlin

Pages 44–45 The Venetian State
p44: *tl*: Gold ducat, BM; *cl*: Scuola Grande di San Marco, eastern view, Venice, SC; *c*: The Doge's Palace, Venice, SC; *cr*: *The Doge Leonardo Loredan*, Giovanni Bellini, NG; *b*: Marciana Library and the Campanile, Venice, Jacopo Sansovino, SC **p45**: *tl*: *Enthroned Madonna and Saints*, Giovanni Bellini, San Zaccaria, Venice/SC; *tr*: Fragment of *Mappemonde*, Musée de la Marine/Mary Evans Picture Library/Explorer; *cr*: pigments and spices; *bl*: *The Marriage at Cana*, Paolo Veronese, ML; *br*: Silk brocade, Museo del Tessuto, Prato/Photo: Nicola Grifoni

Pages 46–47 Titian, master of color
p46: *tl*: Title page, *Dialogo della Pittura*, Lodovico Dolce, BL; *bl, br*: *The Assumption and Coronation of the Virgin*, Titian, Santa Maria dei Frari, Venice, Francesca Turio Bohm/BAL **p47**: *tr, cr, cl* (details), *tl*: *Bacchus and Ariadne*, Titian; *bl*: *The Origin of the Milky Way*, Tintoretto, NG; *br*: *Portrait of a Man*, Titian, NG

Pages 48–49 The High Renaissance
p48: *tl*: *Portrait of Baldassare Castiglione*, Raphael, ML/SC; *br* (detail), *tr*: *The Archangel Raphael with Tobias*, Pietro Perugino, SC; *tc*: *The Apollo Belvedere*, Vatican Museums; *bl*: Title page, *Il Libro del Cortegiano*, Baldassare Castiglione, Biblioteca Medicea Laurenziana, Florence; *bl*: Ducal Palace, Urbino, Spectrum Color Library **p49**: *tl*: *The Garvagh Madonna* – full title, *The Madonna and Child with the Infant Baptist*, Raphael, NG; *cr* (detail), *tr*: *The Battle of Issus*, Albrecht Altdorfer, Alte Pinakothek/Archiv für Kunst und Geschichte, Berlin; *bl*: *Assumption of the Virgin*, Correggio, Parma Cathedral/SC

Pages 50–51 Rome's renewal
p50: *tl*: Woodcut from *Antique Urbis Romae cum Regionibus Simulacrum*, Marco Fabio Calvo, Rome, 1527; *cr*: *Laocoön*, Museo Pio-Clementino, Vatican, Rome/SC; *bl*: *The Triumph of Galatea*, Raphael, Villa Farnesina, Rome/SC; *br*: Villa Farnesina, Rome **p51**: *tl*: Plan of St. Peter's, Bramante, Department of Prints and Drawings, UF/SC; *tr*: *Design of Exterior*, St. Peter's, Vatican, Bramante, on bronze medal by Caradosso, BM; *cr*: St. Peter's, Rome, World Pictures; *bl*: *Tempietto*, Bramante, San Pietro in Montorio, Rome; *br*: Cardinal Bibbiena's apartments, view of Raphael's Loggia, Vatican Museums, Rome

Pages 52–53 Raphael's Vatican rooms
p52: *tr*: *Philosophy*, Raphael, Vatican, Rome, SC. pp52–53: *b*: *The School of Athens*, Raphael, Vatican, Rome, SC **p53**: *tr*: *Pope Julius II*, Raphael, NG; *cr*: *The Liberation of St. Peter from Prison*, Raphael,

Vatican, Rome, SC; *br*: *Parnassus*, Marcantonio Raimondi, The Whitworth Art Gallery, University of Manchester

Pages 54–55 Michelangelo's "divine" powers
p54: *tr*: Monument to Michelangelo (detail), Vasari, Santa Croce, Florence; *c* (detail), *l*: *David*, Michelangelo, Accademia, Florence, SC; *bc*: Marble quarries, Carrara; *br*: Sonnet, *Rime di Michelangelo Buonarotti*, Michelangelo, 1821 edition **p55**: *tl*: *The Doni Tondo*, Michelangelo, UF/SC; *tr*: Entrance Hall, Laurentian Libary, 1524–34, staircase completed 1559, Michelangelo and Bartolomeo, SC; *bl, bc* (detail: *Moses*): *Tomb of Julius II*, Michelangelo, San Pietro in Vincoli, Rome; *br*: *The Crossed-leg Captive*, Michelangelo, Accademia, Florence, SC

Pages 56–57 The Sistine ceiling
p56: *tl*: *The Belvedere Torso*, Museo Pio-Clementino, Vatican, SC; *cl*: *Delphic Sibyl* (before restoration), Michelangelo, SC; *tc*: *The Annunciation*, Pontormo, Santa Felicità, Rome; *bc*: *The Delphic Sibyl* (after restoration), Michelangelo, © Nippon Television Network Corporation 1994 **p57**: *The Sistine ceiling*, Michelangelo, © Nippon Television Network Corporation 1994

Pages 58–59 The North and Italy
p58: *tr*: 18th-century engraving of the Belvedere Court, Photo: Vatican Museums/Ikona; *l*: *Neptune and Amphitrite*, Jan Gossaert, Staatliche Museen zu Berlin, Preussicher Kulturbesitz Gemälde-galerie; *cr*: *Venus Felix and Amor*, Museo Pio-Clementino, Vatican, SC; *br*: *Mars and Venus*, Jacopo de' Barbari, Graphische Sammlung Albertina, Vienna **p59**: *l*: *The Presentation of Christ in the Temple*, Jan van Scorel, KM; *tr*: *A Grotesque Old Woman*, after Quinten Massys, NG; *cr*: *Portrait of Bonifacius Amerbach*, Hans Holbein, Oeffentliche Kunstsammlung, Basel, Kunstmuseum/Photo: Martin Bühler, Basel; *br*: *An Elderly Couple*, Jan Gossaert, NG

Pages 60–61 Mannerism
p60: *tr*: *Self-portrait in a Convex Mirror*, Parmigianino, KM; *bl*: *Cupid Complaining to Venus*, Lucas Cranach the Elder, NG; *br* (detail), *r*: *The Battle of Cascina*, Sangallo, Holkham Hall, Norfolk, England **p61**: *cr* (detail), *tl*: *An Allegory with Venus and Cupid*, Agnolo Bronzino, NG; *tr*: Mask designs, Rosso, engravings by René Boyvin, BM; *c* (detail), *bc*: *Joseph in Egypt*, Ghiberti, MD; *bl*: *Joseph with Jacob in Egypt*, Pontormo, NG

Pages 62–63 Chronology; Glossary
p62: *b*: View of Florence (p12) **p63**: *l* (detail): *The Meeting at the Golden Gate* (p8)

Acknowledgments

Key: *t*: top; *b*: bottom; *c*: center; *l*: left; *r*: right

Photography for Dorling Kindersley:
Alison Harris: **p2**: bc; **p3**: tr; **p3**: cr, cr, br; **p13**: tl, tr, cl, cr, br; **p14**: c, b, cr; **p15**: cr; **p32**: cl; **p54**: tr; **p56**: bl; **p61**: br; **p62**: b Philippe Sebert: **p36**: bl; **p45**: bl Philip Gatward: **p14**: cl; **p56**: bl John Heselrine: **p15**: br; **p48**: tc; **p50**: br; **p51**: bl; **p54**: bc Dave King: **p43**: c

Artworks: James Mills-Hicks: **pp6–7**: c Simon Murrell: **p53**: tl; **p56**: tr

Loan of materials: A.P. Fitzpatrick Art Materials: **p45**: cr G.D. Warder and Sons, Gilders: **p11**: cr

Dorling Kindersley would like to thank:
The staff at the National Gallery, London, especially Erika Langmuir and Jan Green for their help and advice; Steve Russell; and all the curators who helped on this project. Special thanks also to: B.A.R. Carter, for permission to reproduce his geometric overlay of Piero's *Baptism of Christ*; Professor John White, for permission to use his reconstruction of Duccio's *Maestà*; Ben Rubinstein at Cognitive Applications; James Wink for advice and permission to reproduce his model of Leonardo's flying machine; Signora Pelliconi at the Soprintendenza per i beni artistici e storici, Florence; Architetto Fiorini at the Comune di Firenze; Signora Camalinghi at the Comune di Firenze, Direzione dei Musei; Signora dell'Opera del Duomo, Florence. Thanks also to: Sam Cole for his research, and his help on the photo shoot in Florence; Jo Walton, Peter Jones, and Job Rabkin for additional picture research; Susannah Steel for editorial assistance; Mark Johnson Davies for design assistance; James Mills-Hicks for the map; and Hilary Bird for the index.

Author's acknowledgments:
I would like to thank the following people for their help and encouragement with this book: Erika Langmuir at the National Gallery, for attention to detail; Sam Cole, Alison Harris, and David Downie for their enthusiasm and professionalism on the photo shoot in Florence; and Philip Steadman, for advice on perspective.

Thanks are also due to the Eyewitness Art team, in particular Tracy Hambleton-Miles, Julia Harris-Voss, Jo Evans, Simon Murrell, Peter Jones, and my editor, Luisa Caruso. Additional thanks to Keith, Jay, and Louis for their support.

DORLING KINDERSLEY EYEWITNESS BOOKS

1 BIRD
2 ROCKS & MINERALS
3 SKELETON
4 ARMS & ARMOR
5 TREE
6 POND & RIVER
7 BUTTERFLY & MOTH
8 SPORTS
9 SHELL
10 EARLY HUMANS
11 MAMMAL
12 MUSIC
13 DINOSAUR
14 PLANT
15 SEASHORE
16 FLAG
17 INSECT
18 MONEY
23 ANCIENT EGYPT
24 ANCIENT ROME
25 CRYSTAL & GEM
26 REPTILE
31 EXPLORER
32 DOG
33 HORSE
34 FILM
39 TRAIN
40 SHARK
41 AMPHIBIAN
42 ELEPHANT
47 AZTEC, INCA & MAYA
48 BOOK
49 CASTLE
50 VIKING
55 ANCIENT CHINA
56 ARCHEOLOGY
57 ARCTIC & ANTARCTIC
58 BUILDING
59 PIRATE
60 NORTH AMERICAN INDIAN
61 AFRICA
62 OCEAN
63 BATTLE
64 GORILLA, MONKEY & APE
65 MEDIEVAL LIFE
66 FARM
67 SPY
68 RELIGION
69 EAGLE & BIRDS OF PREY
70 WITCHES & MAGIC-MAKERS
71 SPACE EXPLORATION
72 SHIPWRECK